URBAN GARDENING
for beginners

URBAN GARDENING
for beginners

Simple Hacks + Easy Projects for Growing Your Own Food in Small Spaces

MARC THOMA

Illustrations by Alex Asfour

ROCKRIDGE
PRESS

For general information on our other products and services or to obtain technical support, please contact our Customer Care Department within the United States at (866) 744-2665, or outside the United States at (510) 253-0500.

Rockridge Press publishes its books in a variety of electronic and print formats. Some content that appears in print may not be available in electronic books, and vice versa.

Interior and Cover Designer: Jami Spittler
Art Producer: Megan Baggott
Editor: Ada Fung
Production Editor: Ruth Sakata Corley
Illustrations © 2020 Alex Asfour
Author photo by Marc Cacovic

ISBN: Print 978-1-64611-556-3 | eBook 978-1-64611-557-0

R0

*This book is dedicated to my daughter Misaki,
who has her own little veggie garden.*

CONTENTS

INTRODUCTION

Ever since I was a kid, I've been surrounded by fresh homegrown vegetables and fruit. Growing up with German parents, I had a backyard filled with fruit trees and vegetable plants. I even tried growing some corn myself when I was little, only to be devastated one morning when I discovered the raccoons had eaten all the young corn! But it didn't deter me.

When I moved away from home after attending university, I tried growing some vegetables on my apartment's first-floor patio. I didn't have much luck. The overhang of the balcony blocked the sunlight, and I was only able to grow some salad greens. My first house purchase was monumental—not only because I had achieved a personal milestone, but also because I was able to use the small backyard to grow my own food again.

Fast-forward to 2005, when my wife and I first saw our current home. Stepping onto the deck off the kitchen was life changing! We saw an urban backyard filled with fruit trees, an established vegetable garden, and even a greenhouse. So much potential, just waiting for me. Over the years, I've improved, built, and nurtured this food-growing Eden into what we call our "Tranquil Urban Homestead." The garden took a bit of a back seat when our daughter was born in 2013, but four years later I came back in full force, building new raised beds for a vegetable garden that would feed our growing family.

It's so empowering to be able to go out and grab a bowlful of salad leaves and a few tomatoes for dinner. Or to pick a handful of ripe raspberries to throw on top of our breakfast cereal. Although it's hard work, harvesting our own food gives us preservative-free sauces and jams, home-baked (and grown!) goodies such as pies and muffins, and delicious fruit and vegetables that fill up our freezer for the winter.

I want you to benefit from the amazing lifestyle changes that come with growing food at home. You have access to healthier, fresher food that can also save you money. It's better for the environment because your food travels fewer "food miles" to get to your dinner table. It's also an excellent hobby for children. I've used our garden as an opportunity to teach my grade-school daughter where her food comes from and how to grow it. She now has her own little garden where she grows some vegetables every year.

If you've never picked up a trowel before, have no fear. This book is written with you, the beginner, in mind! You'll come away with a basic understanding of how to start and care for your urban garden, whether it's outdoors, indoors, or both. I've also created 10 step-by-step edible gardening projects. They're easy and creative, and some make use of materials you may already have around your house.

Ready to get started? Let's dig in and get growing!

PART 1

URBAN GARDENING
What to Know Before You Grow

Anyone can create an urban garden, even if you only have a small patio, deck, or balcony. And if you are lucky enough to have yard space, you can grow even more! If indoor space is all you have, don't fret—you can grow lettuces and herbs on a spare windowsill or in hanging planters in any room that gets enough sun. You can also buy or build a small hydroponic growing system for your indoor space.

This first part of the book gives you the basic knowledge you need to start an urban garden, whether indoors or outdoors, and explains how to keep your garden going so you can enjoy fresh, healthy homegrown food. Welcome to your urban gardening journey!

CHAPTER 1

Urban Gardening 101

Are you excited to get started? A beginner gardener usually starts by going to the nursery or garden center and spending a lot of money on tools, supplies, plants, and those cute planters that are so hard to resist. It's understandable—it's easy to get excited about growing your own veggies!

But it pays to stop and think a bit about your goals and ensure you understand what is involved in growing your own food at home. And mind-set is a key aspect of achieving success with your urban food garden.

Let's look at some basics first, and then dive into what you need to buy.

Why Grow Your Own Food at Home?

Growing food at home, especially in an urban setting, is becoming more popular as people realize all the benefits of eating homegrown food. If you grow your food using organic methods, you know where your food comes from because you control everything that goes into it, including the kind of seeds or seedlings, water, fertilizer, and soil you use, as well as how you prepare and preserve your harvests.

With the high cost of organic food in the grocery store, growing food at home can actually save you money. The small investment you make in seeds or seedlings, water, and fertilizer each year pays you back in organic veggies and fruit that you don't have to buy. Plus, the work you've invested in growing your own food makes you less likely to throw it away.

Growing plants is also a great hobby that is good for the body and mind; it can ease your stress and provide joy and satisfaction.

Go Organic, Get Creative

This book teaches you how to use organic methods to grow tasty, healthy food. Growing organically means not using synthetic chemicals to control pests and weeds or feed plants. Instead, you use nontoxic, naturally occurring pest repellents, weed control, fertilizers, and soil builders.

An organic urban garden is full of life, such as bees, beneficial insects, and worms. It's an entire ecosystem: the idea is to work with nature instead of against it.

And an urban garden provides lots of opportunities to be creative! Part of living more sustainably with nature includes reducing our waste. Check out the "Hack It" sidebars and projects that use found and recycled materials.

9 Steps to a Successful Urban Garden

Start small. It's easy to get excited and want to grow many different varieties of produce, but if you take on too much, you'll get overwhelmed. In your first year, start off small to get some experience and learn what works for you, and then expand in subsequent years. This is also a less expensive way to get started.

Plan what to grow. When planning what to grow, it's most important to choose food your family will eat and easy crops that don't require much special care. You'll also need to consider your local conditions, such as the season, typical weather, and sun exposure. You can find out more about your local growing zone and typical first and last frost dates by doing an online search on your area.

Figure out the best site. Pick the best site for your garden, whether it's some containers, a raised bed, a sunny area indoors near a window, or a space to put a vertical garden. Be sure to consider how much sun the site gets based on what you plan to grow. You also want your garden to be conveniently located close to a water source, your gardening tools, and your kitchen. To prepare the site, you may need to remove grass, clean up or move old plants, or tidy up your patio, deck, or a sunny spot indoors to make room.

Decide on what you'll grow in. In part 2, you'll learn how to build some easy raised beds or planters. But if you don't have the time or skill level for this, you can buy a raised bed kit and, whether you're growing indoors or outdoors, use individual containers and planters. Even better, you can grow your plants in recycled household containers if you are on a tight budget or want to be more sustainable.

Build quality soil. The quality and health of the soil you use directly affects how well your plants will do. When you are starting out, it's important to buy the right soil and add organic amendments to it over time. This is the basis for what we call "building your soil." Avoid using garden soil for containers; it does not drain well and is often too heavy for containers such as hanging baskets. Instead, use potting soil, which is lighter. If you choose to go hydroponic, you don't even need soil! How much easier can you get?

Plant seedlings or start seeds. For a beginner, buying seedlings at a nursery or garden center is the easiest way to get started. However, if you want to grow a particular variety of veggie that your garden store doesn't have, you can also start your plants by seed. When the seedlings get big enough, you'll transplant them into your raised bed or containers so they can grow big and strong.

Establish a weekly gardening schedule. In order to have success with your urban garden, you need to figure out when you'll have time to work on it. This doesn't have to take all weekend. All you need are a few minutes here and there during the week to keep things going, and then an hour or so on the weekend to do some of the longer tasks. Even if you have a busy lifestyle, basics such as watering, fertilizing, weeding, controlling pests, and pruning won't take up too much of your time. And gardening helps you and your family relax and slow down after a busy day or week.

Deal with problems. You will have to deal with problems in your garden, and you need the right mind-set to deal with them and find solutions. This is the main reason some beginners quit. Plants may get sick, be damaged by local wildlife, struggle in the soil or conditions, or attract pests. This book covers some problems and, more important, the solutions. The important thing is not to get discouraged. Even the most seasoned gardeners run into problems. They have just learned to deal with them.

Harvest! This is the reward for all of your hard work. The first time you pick that fresh tomato or harvest some lettuce leaves for a sandwich is awesome. You do need to check your vegetables as they grow so you don't end up with zucchini the size of a baseball bat! And if you have kids, this is the perfect task to delegate to them—if you can keep them from eating everything on the spot.

Understand Your Local Regulations

You would think that growing food at home would be something that no one would object to. After all, you're doing a good thing, right?

Unfortunately, it's not always so easy. There are rules and regulations you need to follow; otherwise, you risk losing your garden or being fined.

Every city or municipality has certain bylaws that control what you're allowed to do on your property. These cover fence height, accessory buildings, smells and noises, and unsightly premises. Before you start your urban garden, be sure to read through the documents that apply to you.

If you live in a community with a homeowners association (HOA), keep in mind that some don't allow any food gardens, even in the backyard. Check the rules and regulations carefully. If your HOA does allow food gardens, they may be quite specific about the types of beds and containers you're allowed to use so your garden doesn't detract from your neighbors' enjoyment or the aesthetics of the whole neighborhood.

If you rent, check with your landlord before you dig up the whole backyard! You may be restricted to using a balcony, a deck, a patio, or indoor space. If you do get some space in the backyard, keep in mind that one day you may need to move and could lose your plants.

Even if you follow all laws and regulations, sometimes the best thing to do is talk with your neighbors. Let them know some of your plans for growing food and address any of their questions and concerns before you get started. Maybe they'll get the food-growing bug, too!

Match Your Garden to Your Urban Space

This section covers the four types of gardens that work well for most urban spaces. But choosing what kind of garden to plant depends on the urban space you have available, so this section will also discuss the different types of urban spaces and which forms of gardening are the best fit for the space. For example, if you have a small balcony, container and vertical gardening will help you best maximize your growing space.

Best Types of Gardens for Urban Dwellers

These four types of gardens work best for urban spaces.

Container gardens. Container gardening in a small space allows you to easily move containers around if they are in the way or if you want a different look or layout. You can take them with you when you move, which makes them perfect for renters.

Raised bed gardens. This is great for homeowners who are looking for a bit more growing space and something more permanent than a container garden. You can build raised beds on your own or buy them as kits.

Vertical and hanging gardens. If you are very short on space or just want to maximize growing space, go vertical! A vertical garden uses trellises and other supports to grow veggies like beans, cucumbers, and squash. A hanging garden is great for herbs, strawberries, and other small plants such as lettuce.

Hydroponic gardens. If you have only indoor space, you can avoid the mess of soil by growing plants in a soil-less medium and feeding them with a nutrient solution. Many hydroponic systems are also portable, so you can take them with you when you move.

Porches and Patios

The traditional porch or patio has always been a place to unwind and spend time with friends. However, this space is also well suited for a container food garden. Imagine being able to pick a ripe strawberry and eat it while relaxing in a comfortable chair!

Porches are great for hanging baskets, as they tend to have sturdy hanging points. You can hang planters from deck railings as well. Patios can usually support heavier, larger containers that you might not be able to put on a porch or deck.

Keep in mind that a porch's roof might shade heat-loving plants too much and you may need to water them even if you've had rain. On a patio, you may find that plants that don't tolerate too much heat suffer from the sunlight bouncing off concrete or stone.

Balconies, Fire Escapes, and Rooftops

If you rent an apartment or own a condominium, you may be able to grow some food on your balcony, fire escape, or rooftop. You'll be limited to containers, but those are easy to take with you if you move.

In all cases you should check with your landlord or HOA guidelines before you set up your garden. There are usually restrictions, including those related to the weight of your containers.

With limited floor space, growing vertically in containers with a trellis, in hanging baskets, or in tiered planters works well.

For balconies, ensure that when you water, excess water doesn't drip on your neighbor's balcony or patio below.

With fire escapes, remember you can't block emergency access and may be very limited as to where you can place your containers.

Rooftops can get very hot in summer, and you'll need to secure your containers well so they don't topple over in high winds.

Yards

Having a yard—whether it's a backyard, front yard, or side yard—to grow in is probably the best option of all. You usually have more space, which means a better choice of location to maximize sun exposure, resulting in more food.

You can use traditional in-ground beds, raised garden beds, or even containers in a yard. Or mix things up by using some combination of all three!

However, exposing your garden to more of the natural environment comes with some costs. You may end up with damage from burrowing animals or deer or other pests. Your garden will likely require a bit more time and effort. And unless you exclusively stick to containers, you won't be able to take your garden with you if you move.

Indoors

No outdoor space that you can use? Not a problem. Microgreens are a great quick-growing option for indoor gardens. And what can beat the convenience of not having to go outside to pick veggies or fruit?

Of course, you'll be limited to growing in containers, but you also have the choice of growing hydroponically, without soil. Your plants can easily go with you if you move.

Growing plants without the benefit of sunlight, however, can be quite challenging. You'll likely need extra equipment, such as grow lights, unless you have a very sunny room with skylights or lots of south-facing windows.

You also have to protect spaces underneath your plants to avoid damage from over-watering. Humidity indoors from your plants can also cause problems if not controlled.

Common Gardening Terms

Annual. Annuals are plants that live for just one year and need to be replanted (via seeds or seedlings) each year. However, some annuals in warmer climates can last several years as perennials. Most vegetable crops are grown as annuals.

Bolting. This occurs when a plant starts to produce a seed head. A plant may prematurely bolt in hot weather, which may render some plants inedible (they usually become bitter). Grow vegetables that are more prone to bolting (such as lettuce) in the cool seasons of spring and early fall.

Cloche. A cloche is a clear covering over individual plants to protect them from mild frost, help them retain moisture, and give heat-loving plants an earlier start. You can buy or make them from plastic, glass, or other materials.

Coconut coir. A natural material that is a by-product of coconut growing, coconut coir is often used as a more environmentally friendly alternative to peat.

Compost. Compost is living medium, added to soil or on top of soil as a mulch, that contains beneficial organisms. You can make it at home from plant waste, kitchen scraps, leaves, and other organic materials.

Direct seeding. Just like it sounds, this is planting seeds directly in the ground where they will grow, rather than growing them elsewhere to transplant later.

First and last frost dates. These are the dates where, on average, you can expect the first frost of fall/winter and last frost in spring. Check the Resources section (page 150) for a link to information for your area. Plants that can't withstand frost should be planted outdoors after the last frost, and

>

and you should finish harvesting before the first frost. You can also use frost protection, such as a row cover or plant blanket. Every year can be different, so these dates are only guidelines. Keep a careful eye on weather forecasts.

Growing zones. Various public organizations have created maps that designate geographical areas as climate zones. These zones correspond to the minimum temperature you can expect in winter, which affects what you can grow. Check the USDA growing zone map on page 149.

Hydroponic. In this gardening method, usually used indoors, plants grow in a medium such as clay pellets instead of soil, or their roots are suspended in air and they are fed with a nutrient solution.

Mulch. This layer of organic or nonorganic matter sits on top of soil and helps conserve moisture, regulate soil temperature, and suppress weeds. If organic, mulch adds nutrients to the soil as it breaks down.

Organic. This method of growing plants doesn't use any synthetic chemical fertilizers, pesticides, or herbicides. Instead, natural materials and methods control weeds and pests and feed the plants. A variation of this is called veganic, which uses only plant-based material and avoids animal manures, fish emulsion, and blood and bone meals.

Peat. A natural material found in peat bogs, peat is often used to help keep a soil airy and light and retain moisture. Peat use is controversial, as it takes a long time to regenerate compared to alternatives, such as coconut coir.

Perennial. A perennial is a plant that lives for several years and doesn't have to be newly planted each year. Perennial food crops include asparagus, rhubarb, artichoke, many herbs, and most fruit.

Raised bed. A raised bed is an area framed with wood boards on edge, stacked stone, bricks, cinder blocks, or poured concrete. This frame is then filled with a mix of soil, compost, and manure and used to grow plants.

Row cover. A row cover is a clear or translucent covering over a garden bed that helps protect the plants from flying insect pests, birds, outdoor pets, and frost. It's also used to warm up a bed in early spring. Row covers can be made from clear plastic sheeting, a fabric cloth that lets in some light and rain, or a mesh that protects from insect and mammal pests.

Seedlings or transplants. These baby plants are grown from seed and available at nurseries and garden centers. They are the easiest way to get started growing food.

Soil amendments. These natural materials are added to soil to boost nutrients and help feed your plants. Some common soil amendments are steer and chicken manure, bat guano, worm castings, certain types of plant material, or minerals.

Sun exposure. This is the number of hours a spot is exposed to the sun and the intensity of the sunlight. It's critical to match a plant's sun needs to a space's sun exposure for maximum growth and plant health.

What Do I Need?
The Basic Elements of an Urban Garden

This section covers everything you need to grow healthy and productive edible plants in an urban garden.

Soil

Some might view soil as just the medium that holds up the plants. But when you're growing organically, soil is also the source of nutrients, water, and food.

If you have a yard, the native soil might not be the best medium for your garden. For example, your soil could be clay-based (lots of minerals but no drainage) or rocky or hard to dig into. Most urban gardeners have to bring in some soil.

The type of soil you need depends on whether you plan to grow an outdoor raised bed, in containers, or indoors.

For raised beds, a good mix is what's known as triple mix: even thirds of a good-quality topsoil, compost, and usually peat (although coconut coir has become popular as a more sustainable amendment). Sometimes a well-rotted animal manure might also be an ingredient. Although you can fill a raised bed with bagged soil, it can get quite expensive for larger beds, and the bags produce more plastic waste. Instead, order a load of soil from a landscape supplier and have it delivered.

For outdoor and indoor containers, use a lightweight bagged organic potting or container soil. Regular garden soil is heavy and does not drain freely, which causes hanging baskets and containers to get waterlogged and weighty.

For microgreens, you need a sterilized soil for safety reasons. You want to ensure you don't grow any fungi or bring in diseases or pests with garden soil or unsterilized compost.

To figure out how much soil you require for your raised bed or container, you'll need to calculate the volume in cubic feet. This is the length × width × height of your bed or container in feet. Usually, it's best to round this number down, as you don't want to fill the container all the way to the top. For example, a planter that is 6 × 24 × 6 inches (½ × 2 × ½ feet) would need slightly less than ½ cubic foot of soil. You can also use online soil and cubic feet calculators.

Water

Plants need adequate water to grow, especially vegetables and fruits. Knowing how much to water can be challenging for beginners. For outdoor gardens, the general rule is about 1 inch of water a week. If you live in an area that gets regular rain showers, that is usually enough on its own, but if you have a dry spell with no rain, you may have to water your plants. With indoor gardening, you definitely have to water.

Check the soil dampness by sticking your finger in the soil. If it feels damp all the way down by 1 or 2 inches, your plant should be fine. You can also use a moisture meter.

For smaller container plants or hanging baskets, try lifting them. If their weight feels very light, then you have to water, often at least once or even twice a day during dry, hot weather, as they dry out quickly.

Light and Heat

Plants need light for photosynthesis. Too little light stunts growth and keeps plants from flowering and producing fruit. Although some plants can tolerate some shade, most vegetables and fruits require sun for at least six to eight hours every day outdoors and artificial light for at least 14 hours indoors.

Heat is also important. Different plant varieties need different levels of heat, but generally plants that flower and then produce fruit, such as peppers, zucchini, and tomatoes, need warm if not hot temperatures to have a good harvest. Plants that mainly produce leaves or roots, such as carrots, lettuce, spinach, and beets, can survive in the cooler spring or fall or where summers are cool.

Picking the right plants for your climate and season is important. You can help plants along by providing them with protection in the form of greenhouses, cloches, and row covers.

Keeping plants warm enough is typically not as much of an issue with indoor gardening, although too much direct heat in winter or cool air from an air conditioner in summer can cause plants to suffer.

Seeds or Seedlings

Seeds versus seedlings—which is better? In general, if you're an absolute beginner, you may want to start with seedlings that you buy from the nursery or garden center, as seeds take more effort to start and care for. Seedlings are young plants that have already grown big enough to be transplanted safely.

Seedlings take less time and are easier—you can just transplant them to your garden on the same day. If you're growing seedlings from a garden center indoors, make sure they get enough light, as they were likely used to getting lots of natural light in a greenhouse.

However, with seedlings, you're usually limited to popular varieties (depending on what your garden center stocks), whereas you can get almost any variety of plant in seed form. Seeds are also cheaper; you can get a packet of seeds (with 10 to 50 seeds per packet) for the same price as one large transplant or a four-pack of small transplants, so seeds are more economical if you have a large garden.

If you are starting seeds indoors, you need to plan ahead and figure out when to start your seeds, based on how long they need to grow before you can transplant them into your raised bed or into larger containers.

Fertilizer and Compost

Just like animals, plants also need food. In organic gardening, this usually consists of an organic fertilizer and compost.

Although synthetic chemical fertilizers feed plants directly, they are also very strong and can burn plants if applied incorrectly.

Organic methods usually feed the soil rather than the plants. Organic fertilizers act slowly, but they last longer than synthetic fertilizers, so you'll need to use less. They are also less likely to burn plants.

Granular organic fertilizers often contain various rock dusts, alfalfa meal, bone meal, and other natural products. Liquid fertilizers or emulsions, such as fish or seaweed, are materials from fish or seaweed that have been diluted with water.

Compost is often called "black gold" among most organic gardeners. Unlike fertilizer, which is "dead" material, compost is a living medium that contains beneficial organisms such as worms. Worms provide nutrient-rich worm castings that help break down compost and soil. If your soil has a lot of worms in it, you know it's healthy! Bacteria, fungi, and microorganisms you can't see in the compost also help build healthy soil that is great for your plants.

The ideal method (but also the most time-consuming and challenging for beginners) is to create your own compost from waste plants, leaves, kitchen vegetable peelings, and other garden debris. A simple way to do this is to make your own composter outside by standing a cylinder of chicken wire on one end and then staking it down into the ground. Add old plant material, leaves, and kitchen scraps (no meat, dairy, bread, or cooked food), and in several months this will break down into a usable compost.

But you can also buy compost in bags and in bulk if you simply don't have the space for a compost pile.

Food Scraps for Improving Soil and Deterring Pests

Uncooked plant material and kitchen waste are valuable additions to the garden. If you cannot compost, there are other ways to use food waste directly in your garden.

Coffee grounds used in moderation on the soil surface help deter certain pests, such as carrot rust flies and cats. Plus, they feed the soil as they sink into it after watering. You can also make a ground coffee "tea" by putting the grounds in a bucket of water and letting them steep. Then water your plants with the liquid.

When mixed in with soil, well-washed crushed eggshells add calcium and other trace minerals as they break down over time. This helps tomatoes avoid blossom-end rot and stops the tips of some greens from burning. Pulverizing the shells in a food processor or blender can make them work more quickly.

Banana peels (ideally from organic bananas) can be lightly buried next to plants to add nutrients to the soil. They can also deter aphids.

When scattered on the soil surface, organic citrus peels can also deter certain pests, such as cats, aphids, and ants.

Mulch

You will be relying on the soil to maintain your plants' health, so protecting the soil surface is important. Mulch does this quite well by protecting soil from excess moisture evaporation, wind erosion, and temperature fluctuations. It also helps suppress weeds, and when weeds do sprout, they're easier to pull out. Mulch is most effective if you use a thick layer of several inches.

Mulch can be organic or nonorganic. Examples of organic mulches include woodchips, sawdust, straw, cardboard (usually covered by one of the other mulches), ground-up corn husks, leaves, and compost. Nonorganic mulches include gravel, stones, plastic sheeting, and other materials that don't break down easily.

Choosing the Best Plants for Your Urban Garden

As an urban gardener, you're not limited to just growing some lettuces and tomato plant varieties. You can grow most veggies in containers if you don't have space for a large garden, or you can grow microgreens on your kitchen counter for a healthy addition to green smoothies or veggie wraps.

Fruit is not out of reach for an urban gardener. You can grow grapes, for example, against a wall or fence where they don't take up much space. Strawberries don't need a lot of space to grow.

Herbs are generally the easiest type of plant for beginner urban gardeners to grow, as they are hardy in many climates and you can grow many varieties indoors.

The following three tables provide some examples of the top vegetables, fruits, and herbs you can grow in your urban space and information on how to plant and take care of them.

TOP VEGGIES FOR URBAN GROWING

Name	Indoor/Outdoor	Suggested Varieties	Growing Zones	Growing Season(s)
LETTUCE	Both	Grand Rapids, Salad Bowl, Little Gem, Red Salad Bowl	4 to 12	Spring, fall
TOMATOES	Both	Roma, Sweet Million (cherry)	5 to 12	Summer
CUCUMBERS	Both	Patio Snacker, Olympian, Marketmore	4 to 11	Summer
ZUCCHINI	Outdoor	Goldy, Black Beauty, Romanesco	2 to 12	Summer

Spacing	Sun Needs	Water Needs	Care and Harvest Notes
Head: 12 inches Loose-leaf: 8 to 10 inches	Full sun, partial shade	Keep well-watered	Prefers cooler temperatures; for loose-leaf types, harvest outer leaves consistently
24 to 30 inches	Full sun	Water deeply, at least 1 inch per week; avoid watering leaves	Fertilize several times during the growing season; protect tomatoes from late blight under a plastic cover in late summer
9 inches, train on trellis	Full sun	Keep well-watered; avoid watering leaves	Remove cucumbers that don't develop (shriveled); keep picking to keep the plant producing
24 to 36 inches	Full sun	Keep well-watered; avoid watering leaves	Remove zucchini that don't develop (shriveled); pick often and don't allow to grow big (>12 inches long)

TOP VEGGIES FOR URBAN GROWING continued

Name	Indoor/ Outdoor	Suggested Varieties	Growing Zones	Growing Season(s)
PEAS	Outdoor	Little Marvel, Bolero	All zones	Spring, fall
POLE BEANS	Outdoor	Fortex, Matilda	All zones	Summer
GARLIC	Outdoor	Hardneck, softneck	Down to zone 4	Spring, fall, winter
SCALLION	Both	Kincho, Parade	All zones	Spring, summer, fall, winter (with protection)

Spacing	Sun Needs	Water Needs	Care and Harvest Notes
1 to 3 inches	Partial shade	Keep watered but avoid too much as this can rot the pea seeds	Remove tips of young pea shoots (they are edible); harvest pods when they begin to fill out
3 to 4 inches	Full sun	Keep well-watered; avoid watering leaves	Set up a teepee with three stakes tied at the top for beans to climb; harvest when pods are still slender to keep plants producing
4 to 6 inches	Partial shade	Keep well-watered but be careful soil doesn't get waterlogged	Remove edible scape on hardneck garlic; harvest after tops begin to dry
1 to 2 inches	Partial shade	Keep well-watered	Dispose of any leaves that show rust; harvest a few leaves or the whole plant

Name	Indoor/ Outdoor	Suggested Varieties	Growing Zones	Growing Season(s)
BROCCOLI	Outdoor	Everest	3 to 10	Spring, fall, winter
CARROTS	Outdoor	Rainbow blend, Bolero	4 to 10	Spring, fall, winter
MICROGREENS	Both	Sunflower, arugula, blend	Grow indoors in any zone	Grow indoors year-round
SWEET BELL PEPPERS	Both	California Wonder, Hungarian Cheese Blend	4 and up	Summer

Spacing	Sun Needs	Water Needs	Care and Harvest Notes
18 to 24 inches	Full sun	Keep well-watered	Cut head off just before it splits and flowers; plant will grow side shoots
1½ to 4 inches (wider spacing for larger roots)	Full sun	Keep seeds damp while germinating; keep plants well-watered	Thin carrots to final spacing when plants are 1 inch tall; hill up soil to cover roots to avoid a green shoulder
<1 inch	Grow indoors under a grow light to avoid spindly greens	Keep misted but not too wet; a self-watering system is best	Use only sterilized soil and flats; harvest when first leaf pair opens fully and turns green; cut a few times or pull out the whole plant with roots to eat whole
12 to 24 inches	Full sun	Keep soil moist at all times	Pinch back growing tips to encourage more leaf growth to protect against sun scald. Pick when green and firm or leave on until final color is achieved (for maximum Vitamin C content)

TOP FRUITS FOR URBAN GROWING

Name	Indoor/Outdoor	Suggested Varieties	Growing Zones	Growing Season(s)
STRAWBERRIES	Both	Albion, Tillamook, Earliglow	5 to 9	Spring, summer
RASPBERRIES	Outdoor	Summer bearing: Boyne, Cascade Delight Everbearing: Heritage, Caroline Red	3 to 9	Spring, summer, fall
BLUEBERRIES	Outdoor	Bluecrop, Blueray, Bonus	2 to 8	Spring, summer, fall
RHUBARB	Outdoor	Holstein Bloodred, McDonald's Canadian Red	Down to zone 3	Spring, summer

Spacing	Sun Needs	Water Needs	Care and Harvest Notes
18 to 24 inches	Full sun	Avoid watering leaves	Plants produce runners that can be staked to the ground to get baby plants; after about 3 years, get rid of parent plants, as they will be spent; cut down foliage to about 1 inch after main harvest to get a secondary harvest in late summer
18 inches	Full sun	Keep well-watered	Support canes with wire trellis strung between two poles; prune last year's growth (brown canes) to ground and prune this year's to 2 to 3 feet off ground
24 to 30 inches	Partial shade	Keep moderately watered (1 inch per week during growing, up to 4 inches per week while fruiting)	Plant in slightly acidic soil by adding pine needles or aged sawdust as mulch; prune only old wood, as fruit will form on last year's growth
24 to 48 inches	Partial shade	Keep well-watered	Only use stalks, as leaves contain a toxin; remove flower stalks that develop; pair rhubarb with apples, strawberries, and other fruit

Name	Indoor/ Outdoor	Suggested Varieties	Growing Zones	Growing Season(s)
LEMON	Both	Meyer	8 to 11 (in colder zones move indoors in winter)	Year-round (needs to be protected from freezing)
GRAPES	Outdoor	Concord, Thompson, Cotton Candy	3 to 10	Summer
WATERMELON	Both	Black Beauty, Sugar Baby	4 to 10	Summer
CURRANTS	Outdoor	Red: Cascade, Red Lake Black: Boskoop Giant, Titania, Ben Sarek	3 to 8	Summer

Spacing	Sun Needs	Water Needs	Care and Harvest Notes
12 to 25 feet	Full sun	Keep well-watered	Lemons should produce all year long
6 inches or more	Full sun	Keep well-watered, reducing watering slightly during fruiting so that fruit ripens	Do well grown on arbor or trained along wall; grow in containers trained on wooden trellis
24 to 36 inches	Full sun	Keep well-watered	Needs a lot of heat, so plant in greenhouse or under cloche or row cover; pick when tendril nearest fruit withers
4 to 5 feet	Full sun, partial shade (afternoon shade in warm to hot climates)	Keep well-watered	Keep well-mulched to depth of 2 to 4 inches; avoid fertilizers high in nitrogen to discourage disease; keep well-pruned to maintain form

TOP HERBS FOR URBAN GROWING

Name	Indoor/Outdoor	Suggested Varieties	Growing Zones	Growing Season(s)
CHIVES	Both	Common, garlic	3 to 12	Spring, fall
BASIL	Both	Sweet, Genovese, lemon, holy	3 to 10 (but not cold-hardy)	Spring, summer, fall
OREGANO	Both	Greek, Italian, marjoram	Down to zone 5	Summer
ROSEMARY	Both	Arp, Spice Islands, creeping	Up to zone 8	Summer
MINT	Both	Peppermint, spearmint, chocolate, pineapple	Down to zone 5	Spring, fall

Spacing	Sun Needs	Water Needs	Care and Harvest Notes
12 inches	Full sun	Keep evenly watered	Divide clumps in spring or fall; harvest to within 2 inches height
8 to 10 inches	Full sun	Keep well-watered the whole summer	Pinch flower buds and harvest often to make bushier plant
10 inches	Full sun	Keep soil slightly dry between watering	Dries well when harvested
24 to 36 inches	Full sun	Drought tolerant but water well in dry weather	Mulch deeply or move plants into a frost-free area before winter; harvest branches as needed
3 inches	Full sun to heavy shade	Keep soil moist	Don't plant directly in garden—it spreads; plant in pots; clip leaves as needed

Name	Indoor/ Outdoor	Suggested Varieties	Growing Zones	Growing Season(s)
LEMON BALM	Both	Compacta, Aurea	Down to zone 6	Spring, fall
CHAMOMILE	Outdoor	German	2 to 12	Spring, fall
SAGE	Both	Common, golden, purple, tricolor	Down to zone 5	Summer
THYME	Both	English, creeping	Down to zone 4	Spring, summer, fall
CILANTRO (LEAF)/ CORIANDER (SEED)	Both	Vietnamese, Calypso, Santo (for seeds)	2 to 12	Spring, fall, winter

Spacing	Sun Needs	Water Needs	Care and Harvest Notes
3 inches	Partial shade	Keep soil moist	Same as mint
4 to 6 inches	Full sun	Drought tolerant but water well in dry weather	Harvest regularly to prevent self-sowing; gather flowers before they open
12 inches	Full sun	Drought tolerant but water well in dry weather	Trim by a third in spring to get new growth; harvest and dry leaves in an airy spot
9 to 15 inches	Full sun	Drought tolerant but water well in dry weather; damp, cold soil will kill	Trim after flowering; harvest individual leaves or complete stems/branches and dry
2 to 4 inches for leaves, 9 inches for seeds	Partial shade	Water sparingly in dry weather	In winter, protect outdoor plants with cloche; harvest leaves as needed; after it bolts in summer, harvest seeds and dry

Your Urban Garden Tool Kit

This section covers the basic tool kit you need for your urban garden. Any special tools for the projects later in the book are listed there.

The Starter Kit: Basic Tools

Trowel. Use this small handheld shovel to dig holes to transplant seedlings, do basic weeding, or move soil from a bag to a container. Look for a sturdy, well-balanced, and easy-to-grip trowel, because you will use it a lot. Corona makes great hand tools for gardening.

Three-pronged cultivator. Think of this as a sturdy hand with three fingers. The cultivator can be used to do light weeding, work granular fertilizer or compost into the soil, and loosen soil for direct seeding. Look for a strong, well-balanced one with a comfortable handle.

Pruners. A good pair of pruners/pruning shears/secateurs is a necessity. They are usually used to trim plants and bushes, but in a pinch you can use them to cut string or open bags of soil or fertilizer. Just don't use them to cut wire! Look for a good pair that is well-balanced and allows you to change out the blades if they get damaged. Fiskars pruners are a good all-around value.

Watering can/hose. To water your plants, especially in containers, you need a good watering can. If you have raised beds or a lot of containers, you might also want a water hose to save time and effort. The water hose should be easy to handle and not too heavy. You'll also need a spray nozzle with a few different spray settings. The cans from Haws are high quality but a bit expensive.

Hammer. A hammer is handy for knocking plant stakes into the ground or nailing together a trellis. Stanley is a good brand for any kind of woodworking hand tool, such as a hammer.

Gloves. You need gloves to protect your hands when working with prickly branches, such as raspberries or blackberries. Gloves also keep your hands cleaner if you're doing a quick weeding job just before heading out and don't have time to scrub your hands clean. The Watson line of gloves gives you some options.

Container for collecting debris or the harvest. It's nice to have containers to collect garden debris for disposal or collect your harvest so you don't have to make multiple trips to the compost bin or kitchen. You don't necessarily need anything fancy, like a specialized garden trug or basket. You can use an old cardboard box, a garbage can, or a plastic bag.

Spray bottle. A standard spray bottle can be very useful for spraying seed trays if you're raising your own transplants from seeds or growing microgreens, as well as spraying a soap and water solution on aphids if you find them on your plants. You can also use it to cool yourself down in the garden on hot days!

Leveling Up: Specialty and Upgrade Items

Moisture meter. As a beginner, you might not know if you need to water a plant, especially one in a container. A moisture meter has a metal probe that you stick in the soil and a meter at the top with markings that show you the moisture level in the soil, whether dry, damp, or wet.

Grow light. If you're starting your own seeds or growing seedlings or mature plants indoors without adequate natural light, you'll need a grow light. These use fluorescent or LED bulbs that provide the right amount and type of light your plants need. You can buy a grow light on a stand or build your own (see page 72).

Long-handled shovel. If you're gardening in raised beds, you may need to dig something out or move soil around. A large shovel with a long handle saves your back and makes the work go more quickly.

Rake. A rake comes in handy when leveling off the soil before planting or raking up debris in your garden. A standard garden rake (with a rectangular shape) is the most versatile, but you may also want a leaf rake (with a triangular shape) if you have many trees.

Drip irrigation system. Watering your plants at the roots is much more efficient than using sprinklers. A drip system saves time because you can set it on a timer. You can use a drip system for both containers and raised beds. Rain Bird is a brand that produces good-quality kits that provide everything you need to get started.

Grow tent. This can be used to start seeds in spring but also in indoor gardening to provide light and warmth and keep pests away from your plants. It also controls humidity and can be cleaner than growing your plants on the kitchen counter.

CHAPTER 2
Outdoor Urban Gardens

Ready to start growing outdoors? This chapter covers everything you need to know to create and grow the best outdoor food garden.

You'll learn how to find a good spot and plan out what you'll grow to maximize the space you have. You'll get tips on how best to construct your garden, including ways to save money and use recycled materials.

Then you'll learn how to plant your garden and take care of it, including dealing with issues that are specific to outdoor gardens.

Planning Your Outdoor Urban Garden

This section covers everything you need to take into consideration when locating your new outdoor food garden to minimize potential problems.

Picking the Perfect Spot

You may be lucky and have a choice of locations for your garden in your backyard, side yard, or front yard. Or you may have only one spot that works, especially if you live in an apartment or condominium. No matter your situation, here are five important factors to keep in mind when considering a spot so you can tailor what you grow to the conditions of the space you'll be using.

Sun exposure. The sun allows plants to grow via photosynthesis (remember that from science class?) and produce food in large quantities. Heat-loving plants, such as tomatoes, peppers, squash, beans, eggplants, and cucumbers, need at least eight hours of full sun. Most fruit, such as strawberries and grapes, also need full sun for a large part of the day. Other plants, such as broccoli, kale, cauliflower, and cabbage, on the other hand, can do with slightly less sun.

Wind protection. High winds can damage your plants and can bring cold air that affects food production. You might think that solid structures block the wind effectively, but in most cases, the wind simply climbs over top and then comes down the other side at a higher speed, causing damage to the plants. Instead, a semisolid barrier acts as a better windbreak that slows down the wind but still lets it through.

Proximity to water. Your plants need water. Position your garden so it's relatively close to a water source so you don't have to drag a hose through your backyard. If you're lucky and you get consistent rain each week, even in summer, you might need to hand-water only containers that are under cover, such as on a porch or a balcony.

Level ground. It'll be much easier to garden in a level area. Gardening on a slope is a challenge mainly because of water runoff, but you can do a few things to make it work. Use tiered raised beds where one bed's front bottom edge sits on top of the lower bed's top back edge. Avoid putting your garden at the bottom of a slope, as water may pool after heavy rain and your plants may drown.

Accessibility. Locate your garden close to your kitchen so you are more likely to pop out just before dinner to pick some fresh veggies or herbs to cook with. And you want to be able to reach all parts of your garden easily without having to step around obstacles or struggle to reach parts of your garden.

In the Zone: What's Your Growing Season?

It would be great if we could grow year-round anywhere in the world, but the reality is that there are specific growing seasons in different parts of the world. You need to know your growing zone and frost dates, as these determine the growing season you will work with.

If you live in the United States, you can refer to a USDA zone map such as the one at the back of this book (see page 149) to find your growing zone. To find out your first and last frost dates, you can search online by zip code or call your local cooperative extension office. If you live elsewhere, an online search for your area is your best bet.

Maybe your growing season is just a few short months, or maybe you can grow most of the year with only a few winter months when you can only grow cold-hardy crops. Either way, knowing your zone and frost dates is important for the next step in the garden-planning process: choosing what to plant.

Choosing Your Bounty: What to Plant

So, what can you plant? This depends on where you live, the location of your garden, and the type of garden you decide on.

Your growing zone and first and last frost dates govern what you can grow. If your summers are very short, you need to carefully look at the "days to maturity" printed on most seed packages to make sure you'll have enough warm weather with long days for the seeds to grow.

If the only place you can find for your garden gets partial sun throughout the day, you won't have much success with heat-loving crops such as tomatoes, eggplants, peppers, and squash. You may only be able to grow greens such as lettuce, mustard greens, and chard.

If you're only able to garden in containers, your container size dictates what you can grow. Most root crops—those that grow underground, like potatoes, beets, and carrots—need deep soil and won't do well in hanging baskets or tiered containers. You will need enough room to use bigger containers, like five-gallon buckets.

Refer to the plant charts in chapter 1 (starting on page 20) to help you choose what you can grow in your conditions.

Keeping the Garden Going

If you want to increase your harvest, succession planting allows you to grow more in the same amount of space.

The concept is simple. As you harvest mature crops, you plant new ones in their place. The trick is to figure out what plants will still produce before the growing season ends. You want to pick a cool-season crop that finishes producing in early to midsummer and then plant a warm-season crop that can be harvested in late summer or early fall before your first frost date. Or you can plant a more cold-hardy crop that can survive a few frosts. One example is to grow peas in the spring and early summer, followed by tomatoes in the summer, and then maybe radishes in the fall.

Getting Creative with Your Outdoor Garden

Now that you have chosen where to site your outdoor garden, it's time to actually create it! It's important to create the garden that works for your space. You may need to do some do-it-yourself (DIY) projects to best use your space, especially if you want to have a raised bed or vertical/hanging garden and don't want to spend money on more expensive prefabricated structures or kits. The projects in chapter 4 (see page 97) are a good place to start.

Raised Bed Gardens

Raised beds are one of the most popular "containers" for a garden. They do require a bit more space than a container garden and are more permanent, so keep this in mind if you rent or know you will be moving in the near future.

Raised beds can be built from many different materials. The most common is wood, as it is easy to work with and relatively inexpensive. You can have your lumber cut to length at a home center or lumberyard, and then it's just a matter of screwing it together. The raised bed project (see page 103) provides simple step-by-step instructions for how to build one.

Alternative building materials are bricks or cinder/concrete blocks. You can simply stack them up, or make a more permanent bed by cementing them together. If cement intimidates you, try construction adhesive, which comes in a tube and is available online or at home stores.

It's a good idea to line your bed to protect your plants from burrowing mammals, such as gophers and moles. The easiest option is to line the bottom of your garden with fine mesh (sometimes called hardware cloth), attach it to the sides of the bed, and add soil. For smaller wooden raised beds less than 8 square feet, you can put in a solid bottom of planks or plywood. Just remember to drill some drainage holes.

To fill your bed, buy the best-quality triple mix soil you can get. You can buy bags of soil at the garden center, but for larger beds or multiple beds, it's much more cost-effective to have bulk soil delivered. (See page 14 for instructions on calculating how much soil you need.)

In terms of maintenance, raised beds require 1 inch or more of water each week. If it doesn't rain enough, you'll need to water, either by hand with a watering can or hose or with a drip irrigation system. Stay ahead of the weeds by regularly weeding. To save time, try weeding right after a rain or after watering the bed, as weeds pop out of the soil much more easily when it is wet. And keep an eye out for pests and control them as best you can with organic methods.

Adding a layer of compost or mulch yearly helps conserve moisture, inhibit weed growth, and build soil to feed your plants. Keep the overall soil level about 2 to 3 inches below the top of the bed to allow room for mulch.

The best part, of course, is harvesting! A raised bed can produce a lot of veggies and fruit, so be prepared to check it at least every couple of days and harvest what is ready.

Container Gardens

Container gardening is one of the easiest and least expensive ways to get into growing food at home. And it's so easy to move containers around (other than the really large ones) or change them out for others. You can buy wheeled platforms to put under larger containers so you can move them around more easily, as long as they're set on a level, hard surface such as concrete or wood.

In small spaces, maximizing the arrangement of containers is key. Keep sun exposure in mind. Place taller containers or containers that have tall plants behind shorter containers to avoid shading plants too much. But if you have more delicate plants that need protection from cold winds or harsh sun, place them behind other containers that have more hardy plants.

Containers can be made from many materials. The most common is plastic, and this can simply be a large plastic bucket with holes drilled in the bottom. Others include wood, metal, ceramic, terra-cotta, stone, and concrete. Every material has its pros and cons. Plastic is inexpensive and light, but it can look cheap and crack. Metal is more durable but still light. It can rust, however, and has no insulating properties. Wood gives you the flexibility to build containers the size and style you want, but it does rot over time. Ceramic, terra-cotta, stone, or concrete containers are more stylish and are generally heavy enough that they won't topple over in high winds, but they can crack and are not easy to move around once filled with soil and plants.

For containers, use an organic potting soil, which has better drainage properties than the triple mix soil recommended for raised beds. You can use a 1- to 2-inch layer of the same mulch or compost you use in raised beds for your planters.

The key maintenance task for containers is watering. Containers dry out a lot more quickly than raised beds. Check them every day, especially the smaller containers and containers that get a lot of sun. You can water by hand with a watering can, use a hose if you have many containers, or, for the ultimate in convenience, set up a drip irrigation system that waters your containers on a schedule.

Vertical and Hanging Gardens

Why grow vertically? In an urban environment, you usually don't have much space. Just as high-rises in the city are built vertically to offer more living spaces with a smaller footprint, we can do the same for our food gardens.

Certain plants, such as peas, pole beans, squash, melons, cucumbers, and tomatoes, need some kind of support. While you could allow these plants to simply sprawl over the ground, this takes up a lot of space and vegetables or fruit that set on the ground are more susceptible to pests and rot from moist soil. And they're harder to pick!

The most common type of support is a simple wood or metal stake pounded into the ground. Just tie the plants to the stakes with string.

Trellises are flat grids of wood supported vertically by stakes driven into the ground. You can get these at a lumberyard or home center in various sizes, or you can make your own by screwing together a lattice of thin pieces of wood (1-x-1-inch lumber) in a tic-tac-toe pattern.

Tomato cages are another option for containing pepper plants and sprawling tomato plants without tying them to stakes. Tomato cages are better than stakes for tomato plants because the cage supports the branches that get heavy with tomatoes and keep the fruit off the ground. These are readily available for purchase at gardening stores, or see the project in chapter 4 (see page 109) for instructions on how to build one.

Another type of vertical growing method is a hanging garden. This is great for small plants such as strawberries, lettuce, herbs, and cherry tomatoes. It can be as simple as a hanging basket filled with lightweight potting soil. Or build a more elaborate tiered veggie hanger (see page 137), which you can use outdoors, too.

To avoid hitting your head on a hanging basket or planter, use vertical hanging space on a wall or fence. The Hanging Drinks and Dessert Garden project (see page 118) is a great example of how to make underutilized space more productive.

Vertical gardens require the same amount and type of care as other gardens, and you have to to help guide the plants up the vertical support, whether you simply wrap vines around the support or tie the plants loosely to the support with string.

Recycle Your Way to a Container Garden

You don't need to spend lots of money on fancy containers for your garden. Instead, you can repurpose lots of found and recycled materials. Use your creativity to come up with unique ideas or browse online (especially on Pinterest) for inspiration!

For food safety and to stay organic, pick containers that have not held any chemicals or harsh cleaners. Ideally, you want containers that held food. Be sure to wash any container in hot, soapy water to make sure it is clean.

One of the best containers to use, and easiest to find, is a five-gallon bucket. You can buy these new from a home center or plastics supplier, but they are also readily available from restaurants and grocery stores where food is delivered in bulk. The buckets are also great for storing soil and other amendments, such as fertilizer.

Other containers include wooden and plastic crates, plastic storage totes, old garbage cans, reusable grocery shopping bags (either fabric or recycled plastic), an old wheelbarrow or wagon, large pots and pans, dresser drawers, colanders, metal watering troughs (used for live-stock), and anything else that can hold soil!

If the container has perforated sides, such as a milk crate, use inexpensive landscape fabric (sometimes called weed block) to line the container to keep the soil in.

Some people also use large soda bottles, tin cans, egg cartons (mainly to start seedlings), cake pans, and other smaller containers. Keep in mind, though, that the smaller the container, the more watering it requires when it's hot and dry. You need to size the plant to the container, so for small containers, stick with plants such as herbs or lettuce that don't have large roots.

You also want to make sure you can drill drainage holes into the container. For wood or plastic, a regular wood drill bit works. For metal, use a high-speed steel (HSS) bit and a cooling liquid (usually some kind of cutting oil). Ceramic, stone, and other hard materials require a proper ceramic drill bit and, again, some kind of cutting oil.

The number of holes depends on the size of the container. For round containers, the general rule is anything 6 inches in diameter or smaller needs just one hole in the middle. Anything more than 6 inches in diameter requires a central hole and at least three evenly spaced holes in a ring between the center and edge of the container. As the container size grows, or for rectangular or other irregularly shaped containers, drill a hole about every 2 inches. Hole size can vary but is usually in the range of ¼ inch to ⅜ inch.

In order to preserve the surface the container is on and provide a water reservoir to keep the container moist in very dry conditions, add an appropriate-size drip tray or saucer. You can use an old baking sheet for larger containers or old plates or flat takeout containers for smaller ones.

If you're not using a drip tray and plan to place containers on a wood surface, like a deck, make sure to elevate the container on pot feet (or scrap strips of wood) so water doesn't rot the deck surface. Moving the containers periodically also helps keep the deck surface from being constantly wet underneath the containers.

Planting Your Outdoor Garden

After all this preparation, you're finally ready to plant! This section covers how to plant your urban food garden.

Planting Seedlings

The easiest way for a beginner to get started is to buy and transplant seedlings. However, as you become more seasoned, planting seeds is more economical and allows you to grow more varieties of plants.

Ideally, buy your seedlings from a nursery or garden center, where the quality and variety tend to be better than in the plant section of a grocery store or big box store. Choose seedlings that look healthy: not wilted or with too many yellowed leaves. Sometimes it's better to buy small seedlings, as large ones tend to be root-bound, meaning they have outgrown their pot and become stressed, and may have a harder time adjusting when transplanted.

Here are the steps for transplanting seedlings:

1. Pick a day that is overcast or even rainy. If it's a hot, sunny day, transplant late in the day when things have cooled down. Make sure your seedlings are well-watered before transplanting.

2. Prepare the container or the raised bed by adding a small amount of a slow-release organic fertilizer and mixing it into the soil. Make sure the soil is loose and not compacted if planting into the ground.

3. Check the plant spacing using the charts in chapter 1 (starting on page 20) or checking the label in the pot. Dig holes in the container or raised bed at the suggested spacing. Make the holes as deep as the pot the seedling is in.

4. Gently place your open hand over the top of the pot and straddle the stem of the seedling with your fingers to support it. Turn the pot over and tap the

bottom of it with your other hand or tap the pot on the edge of the planting container or raised bed. The seedling should slip out with most of the soil attached to the roots.

5. Put the seedling in the hole and make sure the stem is at the same level in the soil as it was in the pot. An exception to this are tomato plants—you can remove the lower branches and bury the plant to just below the topmost set of leaves. Tomato plants generate more roots from the lowest branches. Firm up the soil around the stem, being careful not to break it.

6. Water the seedlings well so they have a good start, and be sure they get adequate water in their first few days in the garden. Seedlings need 1 inch of water every few days, more if the weather is very dry or windy. You can check the dampness of the seedling by sticking your finger in the top few inches of soil.

Direct Seeding

For some plants, direct seeding makes the most sense and takes the least amount of time. This usually applies to cool-season crops, such as lettuces, and root crops, such as carrots and beets.

Here are the steps for direct seeding:

1. Pick a day that is overcast or even rainy. On a hot, sunny day, seed late in the day.

2. Prepare the container or the raised bed by mixing a small amount of a slow-release organic fertilizer into the soil. Make sure the soil is loose and not compacted.

3. Check the required seed spacing and depth printed on the seed packet.

4. Make shallow furrows to the recommended depth in the soil with a trowel, your finger, or a stick. If you're planting in blocks rather than rows, poke holes at the recommended spacing.

5. Sow the seeds at the spacing recommended on the packet in the furrows, or in the holes you've prepared.

6. Cover the seeds by pinching the soil on either side of the furrow or hole. Sprinkle over more soil if needed, keeping in mind the desired seed depth as noted on the seed packet.

7. Pat down the soil on top of the seeds to make sure there are no air pockets.

8. Water the seed bed well with a fine spray from a watering can or hose. Avoid overwatering, as it can cause the seeds to float away, especially if they are not planted deeply.

9. Keep seeds moist until they germinate. For fine seeds like carrots that are fussy about drying out, put a piece of burlap or an old bedsheet over the top, weighted down and kept damp, until the seeds sprout.

Starting Seeds Indoors

Starting seeds indoors allows you to control the environment the seeds grow in for maximum success. However, it's more work and takes longer. Plants that benefit from starting indoors include all the heat-loving veggies, such as tomatoes, peppers, eggplant, and cucumbers. Other plants can also benefit, especially if you have cool springs and want to give your plants a head start in a controlled environment.

Planning is key for starting seeds early enough that the seedlings are big enough to plant out at the optimal time. Check the days to maturity (from seed) listed on the seed packet or check a seed catalog/guide. Also check how large transplants need to be before you can plant them outside.

Starting seeds requires the following equipment:

- Containers: divided seeding flats from a garden center or shallow (2 to 4 inches) recycled containers, such as toilet paper tubes, egg cartons, or well-washed lidded deli containers

- Tray to hold the containers and collect excess water

- Sterilized potting soil or a soil-less seed starting mix (must be clean—don't use compost or garden soil)

- Watering can with very fine spray or a clean pump sprayer

- Chopstick, pencil, or stick

- Dome or plastic sheet

- Heating mat (optional)

- Grow light

To start your seeds, follow these steps:

1. Pick an indoor spot that is relatively warm. A bright location is best, but if you're using a grow light, that's not as important.

2. Set up a heating mat if you're using one. These are helpful for tomatoes, peppers, eggplant, or other crops that like a lot of heat.

3. Fill your containers with sterilized soil or soil-less mix, leaving ½ inch of space at the top.

4. Place the containers in a tray to capture excess water.

5. Check the seed spacing and depth printed on the seed packet.

6. Poke shallow holes to the recommended depth in the soil with your finger or a stick.

7. Drop a seed into each hole and pinch soil around it or add more soil on top.

8. Water the container well with a fine spray from a watering can or pump sprayer.

9. Set up the grow light over the containers.

10. Keep seeds moist until they germinate, then water the seedlings regularly.

11. Adjust the grow light to keep the light 6 to 12 inches above the seedlings. Check the manufacturer's instructions as well; this distance can vary depending on the light used.

12. Once seedlings are a mature size (compare them with what you'd get at a nursery or garden center), start getting them used to being outdoors (this is called "hardening off") by placing them outdoors in a shady location for an hour and then bringing them back indoors, extending the time outdoors an hour each day for about five days until you are ready to transplant them.

13. Follow the instructions in the previous section (see page 50) for transplanting into the garden or the final containers they will grow in.

Caring for Your Outdoor Garden

Once your garden is planted, you'll need to take care of it. This section gives you the tips you need to grow productive crops while saving time, money, and frustration.

Watering

Watering can be a bit of a mystery for beginners. How do you know how much to water?

Most plants in the ground or in large raised beds need about 1 inch of water a week, whether it is from rain or irrigation. But it really depends on the weather. Hot, dry weather with wind dries out soil more quickly, and if you haven't mulched, this happens even more. Containers ideally need water every day when it is hot and no rain is forecasted. Keep in mind, too, that plants under cover, like those on a porch or in a greenhouse, do not get any rain.

Plants tell you if they need water by wilting. However, some plants naturally wilt during the day and then perk up again at nighttime. The best way to tell if your soil is damp enough is to stick your finger in at a depth of 1 inch or more or dig a small hole with a trowel. The soil should feel damp but not completely waterlogged.

As for watering technique, try to avoid watering the leaves of most fruiting plants, like tomatoes, squash, and cucumbers, as this can introduce diseases such as mildew or blight. You want to water the soil, although greens like lettuce, kale, and chard don't mind getting their leaves wet.

For containers, the same finger test works, or you can use a moisture meter that you stick in the soil. Lift small containers carefully to see if they are light. When watering containers, wait for the water to come out of the drainage holes to ensure the plant is well-watered.

Weeding

Weeds compete with your food plants for moisture, nutrients, and space. Regular weeding keeps them in check.

What is a weed and how do you identify it? Know what your plants look like, and remove anything else. If you planted from seed, study the young foliage of the plants online or consult a seed catalog.

The best time to weed is right after rain or watering. The soil is moist, and the weeds should slip out relatively easily with a bit of help from a trowel or cultivator.

To get rid of most annual weeds that grow from seeds in the ground, cut them at ground level with a sharp hoe or disturb them with a garden rake. You can leave them on the soil surface to decay and feed the soil.

For more deeply rooted weeds, such as dandelion, you need a deep-rooted weeder or trowel to dig out the whole root. Any part of the root left in the ground will likely sprout again.

In terms of prevention, remember to mulch, which reduces the need for weeding and makes it easier to remove weeds that do pop up.

Pruning

Pruning keeps plants in check, especially in tight quarters, and makes plants bushier.

Tomatoes benefit most from pruning. Keep the height in check by pruning off the top stems. (Some gardeners actually stick the pruned stems into soil so they root and produce more tomato plants!) You can also prune the side shoots that grow between the stem and main branches.

Peas benefit when you cut off the young pea shoot tips (these are edible) to produce bushier plants that don't require as much vertical space.

Herbs benefit from pruning (and you can eat the prunings) to keep the plants from getting too spindly and long, which often happens when they are reaching for the light. Just shear off the top of herbs such as oregano and thyme.

For fruit, raspberry canes need to be pruned (the previous year's canes get cut down to the ground in fall or winter) and strawberry plants can be sheared to 1 inch above the ground right after harvesting in midsummer for a second crop. Blueberry bushes can also be pruned, but keep in mind that the fruit grows on last year's wood; be careful what and how much you prune. Last year's wood is typically grayer in color and new wood is brown. You can also mark branches with twist ties or take a photo of the bush each year so you know which branches are a year old or even older.

Harvesting

Harvesting is the prize for taking care of your plants for weeks and months. Time to reap the rewards!

But when can you harvest? The best time is when the veggie, fruit, or herb is at its maximum flavor and readiness. For a general guideline, consult the seed packet or catalog for the days to maturity. But depending on the weather and how much you've fertilized, your plants may be ahead or behind schedule. It's best to use your eyes and sense of touch to determine ripeness and readiness.

For greens, harvest the entire plant or pick the leaves throughout the growing season. In general, young leaves are tender with a very light taste, and more mature leaves are tough but have more flavor.

For root crops, move some of the soil from around the base of the plant to see how wide the root is. Different root vegetables are mature at different sizes. Sometimes the best way to know if they are ready to harvest is to pull one out and see how it looks before pulling out more. If the vegetable is still small, let the rest grow for another week or so before trying again.

For fruiting crops, such as tomatoes and peppers, wait until the fruit changes to the color it should be, depending on the variety. Check the seed packet or plant stake that came with the seedling, or look online or in reference books. Tomatoes should give slightly when you gently press on them and should come off the stem easily. You can pick peppers at any color stage—many go from green to red if you leave them on the plant. Depending on the variety, this may make a difference in taste.

Cold-hardy crops, such as leeks, parsnips, cabbage, and kale, taste sweeter after a few frosts where the temperature goes down to freezing (or colder). These plants turn their starches into sugar to act as an "antifreeze" in these cold temperatures.

For herbs, it's usually a good idea to harvest midmorning, after the dew has evaporated but before the full heat of the day.

Outdoor Garden Issues

Issues and problems will come up, whether it is from insect pests, bad weather, or animals eating your crops. That's the nature of growing plants outdoors.

Common Outdoor Pests

The most common outdoor pests that can affect vegetables, fruits, and herbs are listed in the following table.

Name	Description	Damage Caused	Prevention and Treatment
APHIDS	Small (under ¼ inch) soft-bodied insects in a range of colors, green being the most common	Suck the sap from leaves	Encourage ladybugs by planting flowers (don't buy them!); spray affected plants with a mixture of water and a few drops natural dish soap
CABBAGE WORMS	Green worms that turn into yellow-white moths, often with black markings on wings	Eat broccoli and cabbage leaves	Cover transplants with row covers when planted in early spring to prevent moth from laying eggs; remove covers once weather warms; rely on birds and parasitic wasps to control population; handpick worms and put in bucket of water with a little natural dish soap (to cut surface tension)
CARROT RUST FLIES	Tiny flies that lay eggs that hatch into white worm-like larvae	Lays eggs among carrots and other root crops; larvae tunnel into roots and cause damage	Cover with row covers as with cabbage worms; avoid disturbing carrot foliage, as the scent attracts flies; spread a strong-smelling substance such as coffee grounds
CUTWORMS	Larvae/caterpillars of moths in a variety of colors, depending on species	Eat through a newly planted seedling at the base or even cut it off under the ground	Halve used toilet paper tubes to make collars and place around transplants, buried into soil by 1 inch; spread coffee grounds or eggshells; transplant seedlings later in the season when older

Name	Description	Damage Caused	Prevention and Treatment
SLUGS AND SNAILS	Slimy soft-bodied mollusks (snails have shells) in a range of colors; leave sticky white trails as they crawl; especially prevalent in damp climates where winter and spring are mild and rainy	Eat almost any leaf growing close to the ground	Place cardboard on ground during day; in morning, pick up cardboard and throw slugs and snails attached underneath into bucket of water with a little natural dish soap; set out dishes of beer; spread coffee grounds or eggshells
TOMATO/ TOBACCO HORNWORMS	Large (up to 5 inches) wormlike caterpillars	Feed on tomato leaves and fruit but can also feed on leaves of eggplant, peppers, and potatoes	Handpick and drop in bucket of water with a little natural dish soap; grow basil near tomatoes (may also improve taste of tomatoes)
WHITE FLIES	Soft-bodied, white or yellow-white winged insects similar to aphids; often found on underside of leaves	Eat the leaves of warm-weather plants such as tomatoes, eggplant, and peppers	Blast off plants with water from garden hose; when leaves are dry, use handheld vacuum; spray soapy water on plants

Dealing with the Elements

The weather and elements outdoors can impact your garden. Here are some of the most common weather issues:

Rain. While regular rain showers can keep your garden well-watered, too much rain can cause damage and problems. Make sure all containers have adequate drainage holes and use pot feet or move containers regularly so draining water can't damage the surfaces they rest on. If your garden is in a low spot, rainwater will accumulate, so you might have to add drainage pipes. Rain can cause blight, especially in fall when temperatures are cooler, as raindrops bounce off the soil surface onto the bottoms of the leaves of tomato plants. You can protect your plants with plastic covers and prune off the lower branches and leaves.

Wind. Wind can topple containers or damage trellises and tall plants. Make sure containers are heavy enough (you may need to add some stones to the bottom of top-heavy containers) and well-watered before heavy winds. You can place other containers around them for support. You can also set up windbreaks using well-supported fences or hedges. It's best to have a windbreak that is not solid, as the wind will simply go over the top and come down at a higher speed on the other side.

Sun. While most crops need lots of sun, too much can dry them out and cause leaf burn. Cool-season plants, like broccoli, kale, cauliflower, cabbage, lettuce, and leafy greens, bolt in hot weather, which means they grow a seed stalk and stop producing. Erect shade cloth over the top of sensitive crops. Keeping everything well-watered (especially containers) is important. When planting transplants, be sure to acclimate them gradually to full sun (see page 54).

Cold. Cold can quickly damage heat-loving plants that produce fruit, such as tomatoes, eggplant, and peppers. The sidebar Hack It! Protecting Your Plants (page 62) provides instructions on how to create a protective barrier.

Protecting Your Plants

An easy way to protect your individual plants from munching mammals, such as deer, raccoons, and rabbits, is with a chicken wire cage. Simply fold chicken wire into a cylinder, fold over the top edges to seal it, and bury the bottom edges well into the soil. Add some stakes to secure the cage, if needed.

For a sturdier cage that fits over a large area, assemble a frame of 1-x-1-inch lumber and screws (you can make it the size you need, even large enough to fit over multiple plants), and then staple hardware cloth/mesh to the frame. This is particularly effective against rats and mice that can find their way through chicken wire. You can also use this framework to protect plants in winter from cold by adding a layer of plastic sheeting to the outside. It's portable, so you can easily move it around.

To protect short plants (such as lettuce or other greens) from wind and cold, reuse the large plastic containers that hold baked goods or salad mixes. Remove the lid, then place the overturned container on top of the plants and secure it by placing a few bricks or rocks on the lip. For larger plants, use a clear plastic tote bag. Keep in mind that on hot days the plastic will cook your plants, so prop the covers up to vent them or remove them completely.

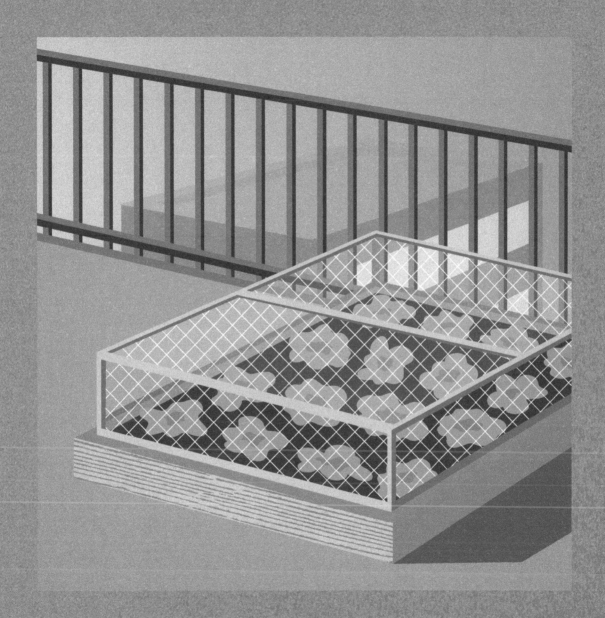

Stop Animals from Eating Your Food

Wild animals will be attracted to your food garden, even in an urban environment. It's easy food for them!

You can use deterrents such as meat meal or bone meal, sprays based on predator urine, and chemicals such as ammonia and mothballs around your planting areas. These may only be temporarily effective, however, as they require regular application. Some deterrents can be dangerous to children and pets if they come in contact with them. If you have youngsters or pets, read the container carefully and avoid anything that could be harmful.

You can also try planting some aromatic plants around your food plants. Mint, lavender, and rosemary can deter some animals.

Physical barriers, while more expensive and somewhat obtrusive, are generally more effective. You can usually block animals that can't climb (such as deer) with an appropriate-size fence. Be sure fencing doesn't violate any bylaws or other regulations in your area. If you can't have a high enough fence (8 feet is the recommended height for deer), you need to obstruct either the runway (where a deer would prepare to jump) in front of the fence or the landing area behind the fence by planting bushes or placing other obstacles.

To keep the plants safe from burrowing animals, such as moles, groundhogs, and gophers, install fine mesh at the bottom of raised beds before you fill them with soil. If you're using wood, make sure to staple the mesh to the sides of the bed.

Fences aren't effective against other mammals, such as raccoons, squirrels, rabbits, and possums, which can either climb them or dig underneath. Block them by erecting a fully enclosed cage made out of 1-inch hardware mesh and a wood frame.

The last alternative is to trap and relocate problematic mammals. You need to first check with your local authorities to find out if you're allowed to trap them. Use humane traps that don't injure the animal, and release the animals only where allowed by law. And be careful: A trapped animal can be vicious.

Outdoor Growing FAQ

Q: I really don't have much time. What are the best time-saving techniques I can use so I'm not in the garden all day on the weekend?

A: Think automation and prevention. For automation, invest in an irrigation system such as a drip irrigation kit. Stick it on a timer and you will rarely need to hand-water, although you should check periodically that it's still working and your plants are getting enough water. For prevention, mulch your soil heavily to cut down on weeding and moisture loss.

Q: Why aren't my plants growing well?

A: There are many possible factors, so let's look at each one individually.

- Is it warm enough for the plants? If not, cover them with row cover or a plastic covering (see page 13). Typically, if there is frost in the morning, you should cover the plants, at least at night.
- Have you fertilized the plants? Water them with a liquid fertilizer, such as seaweed or fish, to give them a quick boost of nutrients. Additionally, scatter some compost or a slow-release granular organic fertilizer around the plant and lightly rake it in. You can apply a liquid fertilizer every two weeks, and slow-release granular fertilizer once a month.
- Are they getting enough water? An inch a week is usually enough, but plants in containers need water daily if it is hot and dry.
- Do they have a disease? Leaves and fruit that are discolored, disfigured, or otherwise different in appearance indicate disease. Disease can also cause plant stems to turn gray or black. You can try to remove diseased leaves and branches, but you may have to remove the entire plant so the disease doesn't spread to other plants.
- Are pests eating your plants? Holes in leaves or fruit indicate pest damage.

Q: Why are my tomatoes/peppers/eggplant/squash getting brown, sunken spots on the bottom?

A: This is called blossom-end rot and is a sign of a lack of calcium in the plant. One possible cause is inconsistent watering. Tomatoes, for example, need consistent water. They should never dry out completely and then get watered heavily; that affects their ability to absorb calcium from the soil. Water consistently and mulch heavily. You can add extra calcium to the soil in the form of crushed eggshells or bone meal. Avoid overfertilizing, especially during early fruiting, when the tomatoes are just forming, and avoid disturbing the roots, as any root damage can affect calcium uptake.

Q: Why are the small squash on my plants turning brown and rotting away before they have a chance to develop fully?

A: This is usually because the blossoms are not getting pollinated. The female flower must be pollinated by a male flower's pollen; bees help distribute pollen when they visit flowers to collect nectar, and pollen blows around on windy days, settling on female flowers in the process. You can help female flowers by hand-pollinating. Gently open a female flower (the flower that has a small swelling on the stem that is the baby squash) and a male flower (without the swelling). Then use a clean paintbrush or cotton swab to grab some pollen from the male flower and deposit it on the female flower.

Q: Is getting a greenhouse worth the expense?

A: If you're really serious about growing food then, yes, it is a wise investment. With a greenhouse, you can start your own seeds in spring without taking up valuable space indoors, protect sensitive plants from the winter cold, and even grow food year-round in areas that have relatively mild winters (zone 8 and above). Check the Resources section (see page 150) for some suggested books.

Q: How can I get my kids involved in growing food?

A: Young children can help you harvest. You may not collect much of particularly tasty fruit like berries: Kids are more likely to put them in their mouth than in the collection container! Give older children (five and older) their own space in the garden. Build a small raised bed for them by completing the project in chapter 4 (see page 103) with shorter lengths of lumber, or help them set up a few containers. Teach them how to plant seeds or transplant seedlings and how to care for the garden.

Q: I have pets (dogs or cats) and they dig up my plants! How can I keep them from doing this?

A: Use some of the control measures discussed earlier in this chapter, such as building cages around your plants. Give your pets their own area of the garden where they can dig in the soil, so they are not tempted to dig up your beds. Make it appealing by providing bones for dogs to bury or catnip for cats to munch on.

CHAPTER 3

Indoor Urban Gardens

Don't have the outdoor space or want to grow food year-round but live in an area that gets too cold in the winter? This chapter covers everything you need to know to create and maintain the best indoor urban food garden.

You'll learn how to find the best spot and plan what you'll grow to meet the unique environment you have indoors. You'll get tips on how to construct your garden, including ways to save money and use recycled materials.

Then you'll plant your garden and learn how to take care of it, including how to deal with issues that are specific to indoor gardens, such as making sure plants get enough light and managing humidity in your planting area.

So let's get started!

Planning Your Indoor Garden

This section covers everything you need to take into consideration when locating your new indoor food garden to minimize future issues.

Assessing Your Space

The same factors that determine where you can grow food outdoors apply to indoors as well: Plants need adequate light, enough water, and the right temperature.

Ideally, you'd find a sunny location so your plants get natural light. For indoor growing, you typically want to mimic natural outdoor light in spring, summer, and fall, with at least six hours of dark, so 14 to 18 hours of light a day is recommended, depending on the season.

Keep in mind that the sun moves throughout the day and the year, so you'll need to pay attention to how much light different areas of your home get at different times of day. If you have trouble finding enough or the right kind of natural light, you can use grow lights (see page 72). You might also want to consider potential damage to furnishings and floor coverings if you plan to leave blinds and curtains open for your plants.

Locating your garden close to the kitchen is convenient for harvesting and watering the plants. Lugging a small watering can around the house on multiple trips from the nearest faucet could be tiring!

You also want to pay attention to the room's temperature. Some locations in your home are not warm enough, such as unfinished basements and rooms that are not heated. And you don't want to put your plants right next to a heat source, such as a heating register, wood stove, or radiator, because they may get too hot.

While you won't have wild animal pests indoors, you still need to consider indoor inhabitants that could damage your indoor garden, such as children or pets.

Making the Space Work for Your Garden

At first, you might think: Great, growing indoors means I don't have to deal with the weather, certain pests, and a limited growing season! However, growing indoors has its own challenges, and you do have to make some effort to modify your space to work for an indoor garden.

The first thing to think about is ventilation. Growing plants in an enclosed space creates extra humidity. You need decent ventilation, but it may not be realistic to open windows in the dead of winter. Instead, you may need to get a portable dehumidifier or install one in your central heating furnace, if you have one. Alternatively, you can also get a heat recovery ventilation system. These are more expensive and require professional installation, but they benefit your home even if you don't have an indoor garden. If you rent your home, obviously you'll need to discuss any installations with your landlord. In this case, a portable dehumidifier may be your best bet.

Hydroponic systems create less humidity, so if it's not feasible to create good ventilation in your home, you may want to use this style of garden.

You'll also be introducing water into an area that isn't designed for it. You may need to lay down a protective layer like plastic tarp on the floor of your growing space or, if feasible, even change out the flooring for something more waterproof. Tile would be best, but even a laminate, vinyl, or engineered hardwood would be easier to mop up when you spill water. You can protect the walls with mildew-inhibiting paint, which is often used in bathrooms.

Light is critical to plant growth. Ideally, you want as many windows and skylights as possible, but that isn't always realistic. If you can't find a room with suitable light, make sure your location has enough electrical outlets in which to plug in grow lights (see page 72). You also might consider installing ground fault circuit interrupter (GFCI) outlets. These special outlets are normally used in damp locations, such as kitchens and bathrooms, and are safer for your growing space because you'll be watering plants so frequently.

Creating Your Own Light

LED grow light stands can be very expensive. Save a little money (and flex your DIY skills) by building your own! The plant strip light kits in particular make it easy, as they eliminate the need for soldering with special connectors and come with adapters that work in your home outlets.

Here is what you'll need for this project:

- Roll of red and blue SMD LED plant strip lights, also called rope lights, with 12-volt adapter
- LED light strip connectors, such as the HitLights 8mm LED light strip connectors or a similar product
- Inexpensive shelving unit or bookcase with open sides
- Aluminum foil
- Wood or cardboard panels (optional)

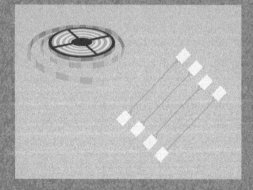

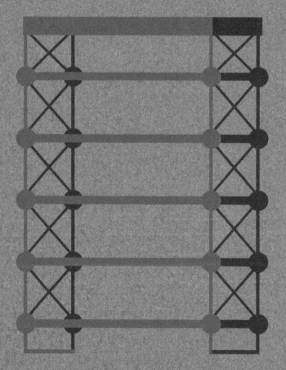

Instructions

1. Cover the underside of the individual shelves with aluminum foil using tape or glue. If your shelves don't have a smooth or solid surface underneath, attach wood or cardboard panels covered in aluminum foil to the underside of the shelf. Adhere these with hot glue or use a fastener, like zip ties.

2. Measure the length of the shelves and cut the LED lights at the indicated locations so you have some extra length hanging down to connect to the shelf beneath (or get longer connector cables). Stick two rows of lights to the aluminum foil on the underside of each shelf (parallel to the long edge of the shelf), with one strip near the front of the shelf and one near the back, so the light is evenly distributed. For wider shelves, you can add more, as long as you space all light strips evenly from front to back. Keep in mind that the self-adhesive on these strip light kits is sometimes not strong enough, so you may need to use additional clear packing tape or stronger double-sided tape.

3. Using the light strip connectors, hook the individual strips of light together so they all connect to the adapter. Voilà! You now have your very own grow light stand. You can also add a timer so you don't have to turn the lights on and off manually (or worry about forgetting to do it).

4. To adjust the distance between the LED lights and the tops of your plants as your plants grow, elevate the containers or flats on wood boards, Styrofoam sheets, or flat cardboard boxes and remove the stands as your plants grow. This will prevent your plants from getting too close to the lights.

Tip: *To make your grow lights sustainable and to save electricity, set up a simple solar panel and battery system into which you can plug your lights. You'll still have the option of powering them from a wall outlet if you don't get enough sunlight.*

The Importance of Timing

The indoor garden growing season is often much longer than the outdoor growing season, especially in climates where winters are very cold. You can grow year-round if you want to.

However, you still need to take into account some timing considerations for growing veggies, herbs, and fruit indoors. Consult the growing zone map at the back of the book (see page 149) or look up when to plant certain plants indoors. Often, you can simply reverse the schedule you'd use in outdoor gardening. For example, in winter, the sun is lower in the horizon in all but the most equatorial regions. This means the sun will shine into windows of your home and provide more light to your plants at various times of the day. Also, any deciduous trees outdoors that usually shade your home will have lost their leaves, so they will no longer cast shade. In summer, you may find that roof overhangs and deciduous trees will shade your windows because the sun is higher in the sky and the trees have leafed out. If you are using grow lights, this obviously may not be as much of a factor.

Heat is another consideration. In winter, you'll likely be heating your home, whereas in summer you may use air conditioning to keep your home cool. Food plants prefer ambient warm temperatures rather than the cool air provided by air conditioning. Keep your plants away from any part of your home that fluctuates too much in temperature, whether from a heater or air conditioning system.

If you also have an outdoor garden, you may find that caring for both an indoor and outdoor garden may be too much work. If you live in an area where the outdoor growing season ends with the onset of cold weather, you can let your outdoor garden rest and start growing indoors to have some homegrown veggies and fruit in winter.

What to Plant

Even with modifications to the light and heat of your indoor spaces, not all plants thrive in indoor conditions, and some plants are not suitable for the limited space you usually have indoors.

Full-size fruit trees and large vegetable plants, such as zucchini and most other squash, take up a lot of room and are not suited to the average indoor garden. Some heat-loving fruiting plants like tomatoes, peppers, eggplant, and melons need a lot of light, which may be cost-prohibitive.

Most herbs grow well indoors, as do vegetables such as lettuces, microgreens, kale, mushrooms, radishes, carrots, potatoes, sweet potatoes, bell peppers, chiles, and beets. Some indoor fruit options are strawberries and certain dwarf fruit trees, including mandarin oranges and lemons.

You need to consider the costs of indoor gardening, too. If you're using grow lights, you will have higher electricity bills. This may not be worth it, depending on what's available in your local markets. Having fresh, tasty, locally grown, clean produce may be worth it, even if it ends up costing more than at the grocery store.

Check out the plant charts in chapter 1 (starting on page 20) for more information on which plants are suitable for both indoor and outdoor growing.

What's the Right Garden Style for Your Space?

Now that you have a good idea of where to put your indoor garden, let's look at some ways you can create the right one for your space.

There are many different ways to construct your indoor garden, and the projects in chapter 5 (see page 123) are only a few examples. You can get creative with your space and come up with an enjoyable garden that meets your needs!

Container Gardens

For indoor gardens, you need to grow your plants in some kind of container. After all, you're not about to put a pile of soil on your floors and plant in that!

Containers are easy to move around as your indoor space changes. You can add containers easily as your needs expand. You can even repurpose the containers when you transition from indoor gardening to outdoor gardening in the summer.

While you can spread out your containers and have them in every room, keeping up with care and maintenance may be a bit more difficult and time-consuming. Ideally, you can group most of your containers in one location.

Maybe that location is a wide windowsill in the kitchen, like the one you need for the Windowsill Salad Garden project (see page 124), or in a spare room. Or maybe you're really lucky and have a sunroom that gets lots of natural sunlight.

Use lighter plastic containers indoors, as a heavy stone or ceramic pot filled with soil may damage floors and will be hard to move.

Plastic containers are usually the least expensive option, but you can recycle buckets or other items to save even more money. You can also get used plant containers in thrift stores or at stores that sell building materials for reuse. Galvanized metal (great for an herb garden) or a wicker basket with a liner are also great choices. You can even match the containers to the rest of your decor.

Indoor containers require a sterilized potting soil mix. Avoid garden soil or compost, which can introduce all kinds of creatures, diseases, and smells into your home. You usually don't need to use mulch, as weeds, moisture loss, and temperature fluctuations are less of a concern inside.

Always ensure your containers have drainage holes and that you have an adequate drip tray underneath to catch excess water.

Indoor containers require less watering than outdoor ones. You don't want too much standing water in drip trays, so you may need to empty them occasionally.

Vertical and Hanging Gardens

Just like outdoors, growing vertically is the key to maximizing your space. Using shelves, tiered hangers, and trellises allows you to grow a lot of food in small spaces. The Tiered Veggie and Herbs Hanging Garden project (see page 137) in chapter 5 shows you how to create a hanging garden indoors. The Microgreens for the Whole Family project (see page 132) triples the square footage of your growing space in a compact shelving unit.

As with other containers, use lightweight soil to avoid making the planters too heavy in your vertical and hanging gardens. It's also important to use sturdy hangers attached to the structural supports of your house, such as the ceiling joists, and to use sturdy shelving units that won't collapse under the weight of your plants.

When watering hanging containers, be especially careful about overwatering. You definitely need a drip tray, and if any water spills onto the floor, wipe it up immediately. Avoid hanging your garden over a carpet!

Hydroponic Gardens

Do you hate the thought of having messy soil in your home? With hydroponics, your plants grow in water instead. Hydroponic gardening uses inert materials to support your plants and nutrient-rich water to keep them fed, replacing the two jobs that soil normally performs.

Usually plants grow faster in hydroponics, as the nutrients are delivered directly to the roots. This means you may get greater yields. Additionally, the water is in a closed system, which means less water use over the life of a plant.

The key to hydroponics is ensuring that none of the containers or equipment promote the growth of algae or molds. In a hydroponic garden, it's generally best for all containers to be black to block light to the nutrient solution. The containers and equipment are made of a nonporous material, such as plastic or glass, because it's easy to clean. You place the plants in rockwool, special clay pebbles, or a synthetic material (such as slices of pool noodles) to keep them upright.

While many plants thrive in a hydroponic garden, those with woody stalks, such as blueberries and fruit trees, generally are not as well suited to it. The easiest plants to grow include lettuces, herbs, greens, strawberries, tomatoes, cucumbers, and peppers.

At first glance, hydroponics can be intimidating for a beginner because of the complex systems of pipes, hoses, and technology like timers and pumps. But you can use something as simple as a mason jar to get started. You need:

- One mason jar per plant, painted black or covered with black tape or a cardboard cylinder to block out light

- Hydroponic nutrients

- Growing cubes, such as rockwool cubes

- Seeds (three per growing cube)

- Net cups (these have slots so the roots can get out) that fit the diameter of the jar (3-inch net cups fit a wide-mouth mason jar)

- Clay pebbles, such as those made by Hydroton, which deliver water and nutrients to the plant

Instructions

1. Insert three seeds into one damp rockwool cube. Start a few so you can pick out the best seedling(s) later. Put these cubes in a shallow container, keep them moist, and place them under a grow light or on a sunny windowsill.

2. Wait until roots start to come out of the cubes.

3. Pick the cube with the best plants (you might have more than one promising cube). Keep the best plant in the cube and remove the other two—it might be safer to snip them off rather than pulling them out.

4. Place a thin layer of clay pebbles in the bottom of the net cup.

5. Put one germinated seed cube in each net cup.

6. Place the net cup in the mason jar.

7. Screw the band of the jar on to keep the cup in place, unless the net cup rim is too big.

8. Mix the nutrients with water per the directions on the container. Pour the nutrient solution into the jar to about ¼ inch above the bottom of the net cup.

9. Sprinkle some more clay pebbles onto the growing cube.

10. Place the jars in a sunny location or under grow lights.

To scale up from mason jars while still avoiding pumps and hoses, try the DIY Hydroponic Garden project (see page 141) in chapter 5. It expands on the mason jar idea with a larger growing space for bigger plants.

Once you get more comfortable with simple forms of hydroponics, you can scale up to bigger, more complex systems. These often involve pumping the nutrient solution past the plant roots on a regular schedule. They require specialized equipment such as pumps, timers, and different plant containers, and they use either vertical towers or horizontal tubes to hold the plants.

Planting and Caring for Your Indoor Garden

In this section you'll learn some specific best practices for indoor gardens and how they differ from their outdoor counterparts.

Planting

You'll most likely be planting all your indoor plants in containers, so a lot of the container gardening advice in chapter 2 (see page 39) applies here, too.

When planting indoor plants, keep enough space between them within the containers. There is less air circulation indoors, and if your plants are crowded you'll have more problems with rot and mildew. Make sure none of the plants in one container or in neighboring containers are touching one another. And, as mentioned, use only sterile potting soil, not garden soil or raw compost.

You also need to be careful about seedlings. Before you bring any seedlings into the house, give them a good rinse to dislodge any insects or eggs.

Finally, at all stages of planting, think clean. Make sure containers, tools, soil, your hands, and the water you use to water your plants are clean. If your plants are exposed to contaminants or disease, they may not produce well or might fail entirely.

Care and Maintenance

Indoor watering is a crucial task. You must do it correctly to avoid problems for your plants and in your home environment. Overwatering is the most common problem, so always water just enough. Your indoor plants are not subjected to wind and direct sun, so they will likely need less water than they would if they were outside.

Weeding is usually not an issue because you're using sterilized potting soil and weed seeds can't be introduced by birds or the wind. Some weeds may come from purchased seedlings that were exposed before they made it to your home, so you still need to keep an eye out. As with outdoor gardening, avoid letting the weeds produce

Speedy Kitchen Gardening with Scraps

Are you frustrated by the idea of buying expensive seedlings and waiting all that time for them to sprout and grow?

You can save money and time by reusing certain kitchen scraps to grow your own food. The root part of many vegetables—the part we usually don't eat—can regrow into a plant that produces new veggies you can eat.

You can't use all kitchen scraps to regrow plants, but this works quite well for vegetables that produce greens you can eat.

It's best to use organic vegetables. Some nonorganic vegetables actually contain a sprout inhibitor. Plus, if you're committed to growing organically, you need to start with organic scraps. Here are three types of kitchen scraps you can regrow at home.

Scallions (Green Onions). You can use the root to grow a new scallion. Cut the scallion as you normally would, but leave 1 to 2 inches of the white section attached to the root end. Place this in a tall, narrow drinking glass and add just enough water to cover the roots but not the white stalk. Place in a sunny windowsill. Keep an eye on the water level, and add more as needed to keep the roots submerged. Refresh the water once a week if it starts getting murky. A new shoot should develop. Alternatively, plant the root in a container with potting soil, making sure the top of the white stalk stays above the soil surface.

>

Celery. Like scallions, regrow celery stalks from the root end. Follow the same instructions as for scallions, but use a shallow dish that can hold enough water to cover the root end. This vegetable should definitely be planted in soil once it has sprouted.

Ginger/Turmeric. These two root crops are similar; both multiply by growing more tubers underground. Take a section of tuber and allow any cuts to heal at room temperature overnight. Then plant the tuber about 1 inch deep in a container of potting soil. When it sprouts, you'll see green tops coming out of the soil. Keep the soil well-moistened but not too wet to avoid rotting the tuber. Both plants produce beautiful blooms, but when you want some ginger or turmeric root, carefully dig up one sprout and leave the rest to multiply. If the container gets too crowded, move some tubers to a new one. The extra plants make a great gift for someone who loves to cook!

seeds. Once seeds get loose in your indoor garden, you'll have more weeds. Remove weeds as soon as you notice them.

With outdoor gardens, you can use any fertilizer, including smelly ones such as manure and fish emulsion. But if you use manure or fish emulsion indoors, you'll likely regret it, and anyone living with you will probably want to throw out all your plants! Use something with a milder odor, such as granular fertilizer or liquid seaweed fertilizer, which still has a slight smell but is much better than fish.

There is really no need to mulch: moisture retention, weed control, and soil temperature regulation are not concerns inside.

Harvesting and Replanting

Harvesting is a joy indoors! Indoor veggies and fruit are cleaner, and some you can eat after just a quick rinse.

The convenience of not having to go outdoors in the rain and cold to harvest something for dinner makes indoor gardening much more comfortable.

Harvesting techniques for indoor gardens are similar to those for the outdoors. You do need to watch your plants more carefully, as they may be ready to harvest sooner than outdoor counterparts, depending on the conditions you have established for your plants.

You can grow in stages indoors using succession planting; that is, replanting new seedlings to replace plants that are done. You can also throw down some seeds around existing plants, and when the seedlings are large enough, remove the adult plants to let the babies grow big.

You can use this method to grow different crops one after another. Keep in mind, though, that replanting and succession planting require fertilizer, ideally a slow-release granular kind. If previous plants had any disease or your soil smells sour, use fresh soil before planting anything new.

Indoor Garden Issues to Look Out For

You might think a controlled indoor environment that is not subjected to weather extremes eliminates problems for your garden. But the fact that an indoor environment is closed can actually cause a few problems. Pests, mold, and that naughty cat can destroy your vegetables!

Common Indoor Pests

Here are some common indoor insect pests that can affect the recommended food crops listed in chapter 1 (see page 20). Always check your plants carefully, especially the bottoms of leaves, for insect infestations.

Name	Description	Plant Affected	Prevention and Treatment
APHIDS	Small (less than ¼ inch) soft-bodied insects in a range of colors, green being most common	Varies based on species but most plants are affected	Avoid introduction by carefully inspecting plants before bringing inside; wear separate clothes for outdoor gardening and take them off indoors; spray soapy water on the plant foliage by adding a few drops of a natural dishwashing liquid to water

Name	Description	Plant Affected	Prevention and Treatment
FUNGUS GNATS	Fruit fly–size gray-black flying insect	Plants that are weak because of other problems	Let soil dry between watering; add a layer of sand to soil surface to prevent egg laying (water from bottom of pot to avoid disturbing sand); cover drainage holes with fine synthetic cloth; trap gnats with yellow sticky cards; place 50-50 cider vinegar and water mix in shallow dish next to the plants; sprinkle diatomaceous earth on the soil surface
MEALYBUGS	Small, oval, seg-mented insects covered with white-gray mealy wax; immature mealybugs are light yellow with no wax coating	Mainly affects avocados and fruits such as lemons, but also fruiting vegetables like tomatoes and peppers	Don't overwater or over-fertilize, as this encourages soft growth and high nitro-gen levels mealybugs prefer; prune out light infestations; hose off plants in the shower or a big sink; spray neem oil (1 oz/gallon of water) every 7 to 14 days until infestation is gone

Name	Description	Plant Affected	Prevention and Treatment
SCALE	Armored or hard type: covered in a hard, spherical armor separate from the body; does not move around on plant Soft type: covered in a soft, waxy film attached to the body; may move slightly on plant; produces honeydew	Trees such as lemons but can affect most food crops	Immediately remove and dispose of infested branches and leaves to avoid egg laying; rub or pick off small infestations by hand; dab individual pests with alcohol-soaked cotton swab to dehydrate; use neem-based leaf shine on light infestations
SPIDER MITES	Tiny, about the size of a printed period	Most annual vegetable crops, peas, beans	Dust the leaves of your plants, as household dust can encourage mites; keep your plants consistently watered (water stress can make your plants more susceptible); prune plants or remove entire infested plants to avoid spread; remove infestations in shower or sink with strong stream of water
THRIPS	Very small (less than 1/25 inch) straw-colored or black, thin; look like tiny dark threads	Many vegetables including onions and tomatoes; attracted to white, yellow, and other light-colored blossoms	Remove plant debris, especially on the soil surface; use blue sticky traps and neem oil; remove infestations in shower or sink with strong stream of water

Mildew and Mold

Moisture is probably the biggest concern when it comes to indoor gardening. Moisture evaporates quickly outside on a dry, sunny day. Wind helps keep air circulating around your outdoor plants, but the air is usually more stagnant indoors. In winter in particular, your plants may quickly develop mildew or mold. The damp air from watering your plants can also cause mildew and mold issues in your house.

Proper plant hygiene helps keep mildew and mold at bay. Remove dead, diseased, and rotten plant foliage and fruits. Keep the surface of the soil clean as well. Prune your plants, if needed, to keep space open between branches, which allows more air circulation, especially with citrus trees and woody herbs.

Watering correctly also helps prevent mildew and mold. Avoid overwatering and empty saucers and drip containers if you see standing water in them. Standing water increases humidity as it evaporates, and your plants' roots may rot if they spend too much time in waterlogged soil.

Wipe up any water spills immediately and avoid misting plants unless you're dealing with disease or pests. Misting puts a lot of water into the air.

Make sure your house has adequate ventilation. Open doors and windows on dry, sunny days and keep the humidity in the house at 40 to 50 percent relative humidity. You might need to run a dehumidifier or a fan to circulate air around your plants.

Here are the most common mildews and molds that can affect indoor plants and how best to treat them.

Powdery mildew. This mildew usually shows up as a white powder, which can develop into a downy white fungus. It affects both indoor and outdoor plants but is more common indoors. If it ends up on your plants, try misting affected plants with a solution of 1 tablespoon of baking soda, ½ teaspoon of liquid soap, and 1 gallon of water. Spray both sides of the foliage. Alternatively, make a milk spray of 1 part organic milk to 9 parts water and spray this once a week on the foliage.

White mold (saprophytic fungus). This usually grows on the surface of the soil as a fuzzy white mold. While the mold alone may not be detrimental to your plants, it's usually a sign of overwatering, lack of ventilation, and bad plant hygiene. The mold can also compete with your plant for nutrients. To remove it, carefully scrape off the mold and discard it in the garbage. Then lightly dust the soil with ground cinnamon, which acts as a natural fungicide. Don't water until the top few inches of soil are dry.

Gray mold (botrytis blight). This shows up as a gray, brown, or tan area on foliage. Over time, it spreads and kills the plant. As always, make sure you're not overwatering and empty any standing water. If you see the first signs of gray mold, remove any affected foliage or even entire plants. Then adjust the environment to reduce moisture and improve air circulation.

Protecting Your Plants from Pets

Although you don't have to worry about outdoor mammal pests with your indoor garden, dogs and cats may see it as a curiosity and a place to play and have some fun!

Some plants can be poisonous to pets, and it's best to check with your veterinarian for a complete list of toxic plants. Common veggies and fruits that are toxic to dogs and cats include onions, garlic, mushrooms, grapes, avocados, and tomatoes (mainly the green ones).

You can spray various repellents to keep your pets away, but many are toxic to pets or could cause discomfort if your pet licks them. The best deterrent is exclusion. Keeping your indoor garden in a separate room behind a closed door, baby gate, or some other kind of barrier is best.

If you have a hanging garden, keep it high enough that your pets can't reach it. You can also put your containers inside a large wire pet crate and keep the door closed. This makes caring and harvesting a bit harder, and it won't work with plants such as tomatoes that expand a lot as they grow.

Sometimes you can distract your pets. Provide cats with their own pot of catnip so they have something of their own to chew on. Give dogs lots of toys and chances to go outdoors to prevent them from digging in your indoor garden.

Indoor Growing FAQ

Q: Why are my plants very thin and leggy?

A: This is usually because they're not getting enough light. Move them to a sunnier place and rotate them regularly so all sides of the plants get sunlight. Add a grow light or two. If you already have a grow light, experiment with moving the light closer to the plants or the plants closer to the light, adjusting the distance as the plants grow taller.

Q: My hydroponic system is very smelly. How can I get rid of the smell and make sure it doesn't happen again?

A: If your system has been running for a while, there may be a buildup of deposits from the nutrient solution in the various equipment. Here are a few ways to avoid the problem and clean it up when it happens:

- Get rid of any dead, diseased, or rotten plants or plant parts.
- Replace the nutrient solution every week with fresh solution, and make sure you use a solution specific to hydroponic growing.
- Use an inert growing medium, not an organic one that can break down over time and harbor bacteria or microbes.
- Cover all containers of nutrient solution so light doesn't get to them; otherwise, algae starts growing. Use black containers whenever possible. If you can't find them, paint your containers black or cover them with black sleeves.
- If these solutions don't work, you may need to empty your system; remove all the plants temporarily; clean the reservoir, pumps, and pipes; and add new, clean nutrient solution.

Q: Why am I not getting any fruit on my tomato/cucumber/eggplant/peppers/citrus trees?

A: Indoor gardens do not have the benefit of bees, ladybugs, and wind to pollinate flowers of fruit-bearing vegetables. You have to act like a bee (costume optional!) and hand-pollinate the flowers. For flowers that self-pollinate, such as tomatoes, eggplant, and peppers, just vibrate the flowers. Lightly shake the supports, container, or plants themselves or vibrate them with an electric toothbrush. Do this daily while the plants are flowering. For plants that have male and female flowers, like cucumbers or melons, first identify the male flowers—those that don't have a nodule that develops into fruit. Use a clean toothbrush, cotton swab, or paintbrush to carefully dab into the male flower to get some dustlike pollen. Then carefully transfer the pollen to a female flower, which is the flower with a swollen nodule at the base.

Q: If I want to move my indoor plants outdoors to continue to grow over the summer, what do I need to consider?

A: The main issue is hardening them off. Gradually move them outdoors as described in the section on starting seeds indoors in chapter 2 (see page 54). And make sure all danger of frost has passed.

PART 2

GROW-IT-YOURSELF:
10 Urban Gardening Projects

Now that you're raring to go, let's look at some easy projects you can create in just an evening or a few hours over the weekend.

Each project has a general cost and difficulty rating, so you can gauge which one is on the cheaper end or which might be better suited for someone with some DIY experience. To start, pick just a couple of projects that meet your needs, interests, and ability. Over time, tackle the other ones, expand existing projects, or modify them for different plants.

A few of the projects involve woodworking and using power tools like drills. Use the appropriate safety equipment, such as safety glasses, when drilling and sawing, and make sure to put away tools safely once you're done, especially if you have kids and pets.

CHAPTER 4

Outdoor Gardening Projects

LETTUCE

BASIL

BASIL

LETTUCE

LETTUCE

TOMATO

BASIL

PROJECT 1
Salad in a Container

Stop spending money on those expensive prepackaged salads! Grow all the ingredients you need for a healthy salad in a compact, portable, self-contained garden. Place it steps from your kitchen, so you can easily pick fresh veggies for your lunchtime salad at work or school. This project is quick and easy to make, using commonly found materials and seedlings of salad favorites. The basil not only beautifully complements the tomatoes in a caprese salad, but also helps repel flying pests. You can use a container made of plastic, fabric, ceramic, or terra-cotta. Make sure to drill drainage holes if there are none, and wear safety glasses while doing so.

Materials

1 container (14 or more inches in diameter and 12 to 16 inches deep)

3 cubic feet potting soil

Organic slow-release granular fertilizer

1 (4-foot) wooden stake or bamboo pole

Plant ties or string

1 small bag undyed woodchip mulch

1 saucer or other flat tray (at least 1 inch deep and wider than the bottom of the container)

Organic liquid fish or seaweed fertilizer

Tools

Electric drill and ⅜-inch drill bit (optional)

Safety glasses (optional)

Trowel

Plants

1 cherry tomato seedling, such as Sweet Million

3 lettuce seedlings, such as Grand Rapids and Salad Bowl

3 basil seedlings, such as sweet and Genovese

Step-by-Step Method

1. If your container doesn't have any holes, use the drill and bit to drill 5 to 6 holes in the bottom. For a ceramic planter, it's best to choose one with holes, but use a ceramic drill bit and water as a coolant if necessary. Wear safety glasses when drilling.

2. Fill the container with soil to about 1 inch from the top rim.

3. Add 1 cup of granular fertilizer and mix it into the soil with the trowel.

4. Make a hole in the middle of the soil and place the tomato seedling in it. Carefully snap off any lower branches, then bury the plant up to the topmost group of branches. Firm the soil around it well.

5. A couple of inches away from the main stem of the tomato plant, stick the stake into the soil and tie the plant loosely to the stake with the plant ties.

6. Plant the lettuce seedlings at the same level as in the pot they came in, staggering them in a triangle shape around the tomato seedling and keeping them evenly spaced from one another.

7. Plant the basil seedlings between the lettuce seedlings at the same level as in the pot they came in.

8. Add mulch around all the plants to conserve moisture and control weeds.

9. Place the container into the saucer. Dilute the liquid fertilizer with water according to package instructions, then water the garden well to give it a good head start. Place the garden in a sunny location.

Care

Water the soil deeply once or twice a week, depending on how warm and dry the weather is. Every two weeks, water with a diluted water-fertilizer mix. Alternatively, add ½ cup of granular fertilizer once a month and dig it shallowly into the soil.

If the lettuce bolts, replace it with new seedlings or seeds.

Keep tying the tomato plant to the stake as necessary to prevent it from flopping over, but make sure the ties are not too tight so they don't choke the plant. Tomato plants benefit from pruning. Prune the suckers that sprout between a main branch and the stem. Prune the lowest branches to provide the lettuce and basil more space and to avoid soil getting onto the tomato leaves, which can promote diseases such as blight.

Harvest

The lettuce should be ready to harvest in as little as two weeks. Harvest leaves from the outside first, rather than the whole head. As the weather gets warmer, harvest mature heads before they produce flowers, and plant new seedlings.

Harvest basil leaves anytime. Cut whole stems to encourage new shoots and bushiness. Cut any developing flower/seed heads to keep the plant's energy in producing leaves. You can also pick the basil and dry it if you have too much.

Tomatoes should be ready 8 to 10 weeks after planting. Yellow tomato blossoms form and turn into tomatoes. Wait to pick the tomatoes until they are a bit soft to the touch and deep red (for the suggested variety) or the ripe color of your variety. They should come off easily with a gentle tug.

Substitution Tip: *This is a versatile project. Feel free to plant a pepper seedling instead of the tomato plant, or plant oregano or thyme instead of basil. Alternatively, to save some money or grow a variety you can't find as seedlings, sow seeds for the lettuce and basil—just add a few weeks to the harvest estimations (see chart starting on page 20).*

PROJECT 2
Raised Bed Veggie Garden for the Family

This sturdy, easy-to-build raised garden bed is perfect for beginners. This is just one way you can fill your raised bed; feel free to plant what your family likes to eat or experiment with a different theme each year—pizza garden, anyone?

Not a DIY master? Not to worry—you can have the lumber for the raised bed cut to size at a lumberyard or home center. If you can't afford the recommended lumber, buy common pine, fir, or spruce lumber, or whatever is local to your area. Avoid using pressure-treated lumber; it requires special handling so you don't breathe in the sawdust from sawing and drilling, and you can't burn the scraps.

Materials

3 (8-foot, ⁵⁄₄-×-6-inch) cedar, redwood, or hemlock deck boards, 1 halved to get 2 (4-foot) pieces

2 (8-foot, 2-×-2-inch) cedar, redwood, or hemlock lumber

6 (8-foot, 1-×-1-inch) cedar, redwood, or hemlock lumber, 3 halved to get 6 (4-foot) pieces

12 (#8 × 2½-inch) coated deck screws for non-pressure-treated wood

18 (#8 × 1¼-inch) coated deck screws for non-pressure-treated wood

6 bricks or cement pavers (optional)

16 cubic feet triple mix soil

Organic slow-release granular fertilizer

Organic fish or seaweed emulsion

2 (2-cubic-foot) bags undyed woodchip mulch

Tools

Miter saw, circular saw, or handsaw

Safety glasses

Electric drill and $^{11}/_{64}$-inch drill bit

Screwdriver bit to fit the wood screws

Carpenter's level

Shovel

Measuring tape

Rake

Plants

6 pea seedlings, such as Little Marvel and Bolero

3 Bluecrop blueberry plants

6 English thyme plants

1 Goldy zucchini seedling

1 Black Beauty or Romanesco zucchini seedling

4 Everest broccoli seedlings

3 cucumber seedlings, such as Patio Snacker and Marketmore

1 packet rainbow blend carrot seeds

Step-by-Step Method

To prepare the area

1. Remove any plants or grass in the area where you are placing the raised bed.

2. Level the area as best you can by removing excess soil or adding soil in low spots. Don't worry too much about the middle, just the edges.

To build the raised bed

1. If cutting lumber yourself, cut the deck boards and lumber to length with a saw. Wear safety glasses when sawing.

2. Stand up the 4 deck boards on their long edges in a rectangle shape with the short (4-foot) boards on both ends.

3. Use the drill and bit to drill 2 holes on each end of the faces of the short boards about 1 inch from the bottom and top and ½ inch in from the ends. Don't drill any holes in the long boards. Wear safety glasses when drilling.

4. Use the 2½-inch deck screws and drill fitted with a screwdriver bit to fasten the short boards into the ends of the long boards, making sure the tops of the long boards are even and the short boards are even with the sides of the long boards.

5. Use the level and shovel to level the bed as best you can. Focus on the corners of the bed and the middle of the long sides.

6. If using the bricks, place them on the ground underneath each corner of the bed and in the middle of each long side. It's best to dig a shallow hole for each brick to sink into until it's almost level with the surrounding soil. The bricks make it a bit easier to level the bed and protect the wood from sitting directly on the soil.

To build and attach the trellis

1. Lay out the 2 × 2s parallel on a flat surface, such as a garage or driveway, about 48 inches apart.

2. Use the drill and bit to drill 2 holes at one end of each 2 × 2, 1 inch from the bottom and 3½ inches up from the end. This is the bottom of the trellis where it's attached to the raised bed.

3. Drill holes on each end of the 1 × 1s about ¾ inch in from the end and centered on the width.

4. Lay out the short (4-foot) 1 × 1s perpendicularly on top of the 2 × 2s. Space them about 16 inches apart starting at the top of the 2 × 2s (the opposite end from where you drilled the holes in step 2).

5. Fasten the 1 × 1s into the 2 × 2s using the 1¼-inch deck screws.

6. Lay out the long (8-foot) 1 × 1s underneath the short 1 × 1s, parallel to the 2 × 2s. Space them out evenly, about 12 inches apart.

7. Drill holes through the top and bottom short 1 × 1s at the intersection points.

8. Using the drill fitted with a screwdriver bit, screw the top and bottom short 1 × 1s to the long 1 × 1s underneath. You don't need to screw into the other 1 × 1s.

9. Use the remaining 4 (2½-inch) deck screws to attach the trellis to the inside of one of the long sides of the raised bed.

To plant the raised bed

1. Fill the bed with the soil. Use the rake to smooth it out. Give it a good watering.

2. Plant the peas, blueberries, and thyme in the bed at the same level as in the pots they came in, positioned according to the illustration (see page 102). Make holes for the zucchini, broccoli, and cucumbers in the bed (see illustration on page 102). Add some granular fertilizer to the holes, then plant them at the same level as in the pots they came in.

3. Sow the carrot seeds along one side of the bed (see page 102), then cover them very lightly with a layer of soil (¼ inch or less). Dilute the liquid fertilizer with water according to package instructions, then water the garden well to give it a good head start.

4. Layer the mulch around the plants, keeping it about 1 inch from the stems. Avoid the area where you planted the carrot seeds.

Care

The raised bed needs about 1 inch of water a week. If it doesn't rain, hand-water with a watering can or hose, or check out the Care Tip (see page 108) to automate watering.

Every month, water with the diluted water-fertilizer mix. If you're not using liquid fertilizer, lightly dig ½ cup of granular fertilizer into the soil around the plants.

Weed the bed regularly as needed.

As the peas and cucumbers grow, you may need to help them climb up the trellis. Wrap the tendrils around and through the trellis and the vines will continue to wrap themselves as they climb.

Blueberries benefit from pruning. Avoid pruning too much of the current wood, as next year's blueberries fruit on this year's wood. Last year's wood is gray and new wood is brown. Remove dead, damaged, or diseased branches. Keep the bush airy by pruning any inward-growing branches.

The thyme hedge benefits from a good pruning in fall or anytime it gets unruly.

Harvest

Different plants are ready to harvest at different times. Here are rough guidelines to know when each one is ready.

- Peas: Look for fat pods. Pick them as soon as they have swelled, which encourages more production and avoids mealy peas. Cut them with scissors or pruners to avoid damaging the plant.

- Cucumbers: Pick them when they are 6 to 8 inches long.

- Zucchini: Keep a close eye on them to avoid growing zucchini the size of baseball bats. They taste better smaller, so pick them when they are 8 to 12 inches long. You can usually twist them off the plant.

- Broccoli: Wait until the head gets to a decent size. Cut off the head with a knife just before the flowers start to open, and leave the rest of the plant in place. You can then harvest the side shoots as they grow from the sides of the stalk by simply snapping them off.

- Carrots: As the foliage grows, check the carrrots carefully by removing some soil from around the base of the plant to expose the top of the root. If the root's diameter is 1 inch or more, pull the carrot. Your soil should be loose enough for you to pull out the carrots without using a trowel or garden fork.

- Thyme: Pick sprigs as needed.

- Blueberries: Wait until the berries get dark blue and are plump.

Care Tip: *To save time watering, add a drip irrigation kit and use a timer or manually turn on the system every day for 15 to 20 minutes.*

PROJECT 3
Wood Crate Tomato Planter with Support Cage

This is a compact planter for one tomato plant and a couple of basil plants. It uses an inexpensive wood crate with an easy-to-build cage that supports the tomato plant as it grows. Say goodbye to broken branches that collapse from the weight of the fruit! This planter gives you easy access to the tomatoes for harvesting and you can paint or stain it to fit your taste.

Materials

Wood stain (optional)

1 (18-x-12½-x-9½-inch) wooden crate

1 roll black landscape cloth

2 (8 foot, 2-x-2-inch) cedar, redwood, or hemlock lumber, halved to get 4 (4-foot) pieces

8 (#8 × 1¼-inch) coated deck screws for non-pressure-treated wood

1 (1¼-cubic-foot) bag organic container or potting soil

Organic slow-release granular fertilizer

Organic liquid fish or seaweed fertilizer

1 small bag undyed woodchip mulch

20 feet strong twine, such as jute

Tools

Electric drill and ¹¹⁄₆₄-inch drill bit

Safety glasses

Screwdriver bit to fit the wood screws

Measuring tape

Plants

1 tomato seedling, such as Roma or Siletz

2 basil seedlings, such as sweet or Genovese

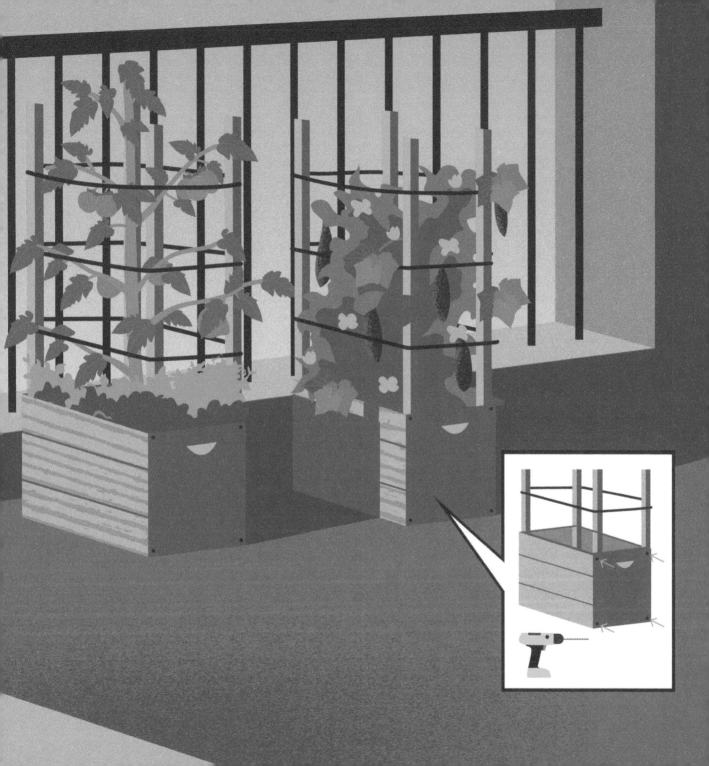

Step-by-Step Method

To prep the crate

1. If staining the crate, stain only the outside.

2. On each of the solid end pieces of the crate, use the drill and bit to drill 2 holes ¾ inch in from the sides and 2 inches from the top. Drill another 2 holes ¾ inch from the sides and 2 inches from the bottom. You should have 4 holes in total on each end piece. Wear safety glasses when drilling.

3. Cut a piece of landscape cloth to about 2 inches larger than the bottom of the crate on all sides. Lay it on the inside bottom of the crate with the excess going up the sides.

4. Cut another piece of landscape cloth to the height of the crate and long enough to wrap around the box with about 6 inches of overlap.

5. Stand the strip of cloth around the sides on the inside of the crate. Make sure the overlap is in a corner so you can secure it easily during the next few steps.

To build the cage

1. Place each of the 2 × 2s in a corner of the crate. They should stick up above the top of the crate.

2. Going from the outside of the crate in, place the deck screws through the drilled holes and use the drill fitted with a screwdriver bit to fasten the crate to the 2 × 2s, making sure they are tight in the corners. The landscape cloth should be sandwiched between the crate and the 2 × 2s.

3. If desired, stain the 2 × 2s to match the crate, making sure to stain the tops only (not the bottom sections that will be covered in soil).

To plant the crate

1. Pour the soil into the crate. Add 1 or 2 cups of the granular fertilizer and mix it into the soil.

2. Transplant the tomato plant into the middle of the crate. Remove the bottom branches and plant it deep, up to the next group of branches. This generates more roots at the bottom.

3. Plant one basil plant on each side of the tomato plant at the same level as in the pots they came in.

4. Dilute the liquid fertilizer with water according to package instructions, then water the garden well to give it a good head start.

5. Add mulch around all the plants to conserve moisture and control weeds.

6. Wrap the twine around the 2 × 2s to create a cage, keeping each strand of twine 6 to 10 inches apart as you wind it around.

Care

Water the soil deeply once or twice a week. Water more when it's hot and dry and less when it's cool or wet. Every two weeks, water with a diluted water-fertilizer mix.

Tomato plants benefit from pruning. Prune the suckers that sprout between a main branch and the stem. Prune the lowest branches to provide the basil more space and to avoid getting soil on the tomato leaves, which can promote diseases such as blight.

If any weeds pop up, pull them out.

Harvest

Harvest basil leaves anytime. Cut whole stems to encourage new shoots and bushiness.

Yellow tomato blossoms form and turn into tomatoes. Wait to pick the tomatoes until they are a bit soft to the touch and deep red (for the suggested variety) or the ripe color of your variety. They should come off easily with a gentle tug.

Substitution Tip: *You can grow cucumbers instead of tomatoes in this crate planter. Train the cucumber vines up the string so they grow vertically.*

PROJECT 4

Bin Bean Arbor

Maximize your growing space by growing climbing beans on a sturdy bean arbor made from easy-to-find, inexpensive storage bins and a roll of hardware mesh. Beans fill out the arbor and provide a bounty all summer long. You'll have leftover fencing from this project, so if you have the space, you can lengthen your arbor by adding another set of bins and mesh. Plant herbs or lettuces in the space remaining in the bins to get even more food from this project.

Materials

2 (25- to 30-gallon) plastic storage bins

Pieces of scrap wood or cement/stone pavers (optional, for leveling purposes)

9 cubic feet organic container or potting soil

1 (3-x-50-foot) 14-gauge welded wire fence with 2-x-4-inch mesh

1 (50-foot) roll galvanized steel wire

Organic slow-release granular fertilizer

Organic liquid fish or seaweed fertilizer

1 small bag undyed woodchip mulch or dried leaves

Tools

Electric drill and 11/64-inch drill bit

Safety glasses

Wire cutters and pliers

Trowel

Plants

8 to 10 pole bean plants or 1 bag pole bean seeds, such as Fortex and Matilda

Step-by-Step Method

To build the arbor

1. Using the drill and bit, drill 6 to 8 holes in the bottom of each bin for drainage. Wear safety glasses while drilling.

2. Arrange the bins in the location you have chosen, such as on a patio or level bare ground or grass. Place the bins 2 to 3 feet away from each other with their long sides parallel, creating a narrow walkway between them. If you place them on a patio or other hard surface (not soil), place the lid, top-side up, underneath the bins so it acts as a drip tray. If the location for your bins is not level, place pieces of wood under the lower part of the bins to level them.

3. Fill the bins with soil.

4. Using wire cutters, cut a 20- to 25-foot length of steel wire. Use the wire to attach one end of the fencing panel to the exterior of one bin on the side facing the other bin by wrapping the wire around the bin and fencing a few times, weaving it through bottom of the fencing panel. Then twist together the ends of the wire, to ensure the pointy ends don't stick out.

5. Bend the fencing panel over to the second bin, aiming for an arch that is about 6 feet high. Cut the fencing to the right length.

6. Repeat step 4 to attach the fencing to the outside of the second bin.

7. Add 2 cups of granular fertilizer to each bin and mix it into the soil with the trowel.

To plant the arbor

1. Plant the bean seedlings at the same level as in the pots they came in, in an evenly spaced row next to the trellis in each bin. Firm the soil well around each plant. Alternatively, plant seeds about 2 inches apart. Bean seeds are usually planted 1 inch deep, but follow the instructions on the seed packet.

2. Dilute the liquid fertilizer with water according to package instructions, then water the garden well to give it a good head start.

3. Add mulch on top to conserve moisture and reduce weeds.

Care

As the beans grow, you may need to help them climb up the trellis. Usually, you don't need to tie them on—just guide their tendrils in the direction you want them to go. The two rows of beans should eventually meet in the middle of the trellis as the vines grow.

Water the soil deeply once or twice a week, depending on how warm and dry the weather is. Every two weeks, water with the diluted water-fertilizer mix. Alternatively, if you're not using the liquid fertilizer, lightly dig ½ cup of granular fertilizer into the soil around the plants. If any weeds pop up, pull them out.

Harvest

Bean plants usually take about 60 days to mature. Once you start seeing decent-size pods, pick them. The beans inside should be plump. Pick every two to three days to keep the pods from getting stringy and, more important, to keep the plants producing.

Toward the end of the season, leave some pods on the plant until they dry up, then pick them for seeds for the next year.

Substitution Tip: *If you have a mild spring, plant peas first in late winter/early spring, and once they are done, plant beans in early summer. Instead of pole beans, try a drying bean that climbs, such as Borlotti, which you can store in your pantry and use in soups and stews in the winter. Follow the same steps to plant these.*

PROJECT 5
Hanging Drinks and Dessert Garden

Grow everything you need to create and garnish delicious desserts or refreshing fla-vored waters and cocktails in one repurposed hanging shoe organizer. This project uses an inexpensive hanging shoe rack with individual pockets, which make excellent containers for strawberries, mint, and lemon balm for topping ice creams, flavoring cakes, and garnishing drinks. But don't feel limited—there's no better way to start your morning than by topping your yogurt or cereal with some freshly picked strawber-ries! Growing the strawberries off the ground keeps them away from slugs, snails, and excess moisture that can damage them. And the pockets keep the mint and lemon balm contained so they don't take over your entire garden.

Materials

1 (66-x-20-inch) over-the-door 24-pocket mesh shoe organizer with eyelets and hangers

3 to 5 (#8 x 1¼-inch) coated deck screws (optional, check the Step-by-Step Method)

1 (24-x-1-x-2-inch) wood strip (optional, check the Step-by-Step Method)

1 (24-inch) shallow trough or planter

1 (1-cubic-foot) bag organic container or potting soil

Tools

Electric drill and ¹¹⁄₆₄-inch drill bit (optional)

Screwdriver bit to fit the wood screws (optional)

Safety glasses (optional)

Plants

12 strawberry seedlings, such as Albion, Tillamook, and Earliglow

6 peppermint seedlings

6 lemon balm seedlings, such as Compacta and Aurea

PEPPERMINT ·········· STRAWBERRIES

·········· LEMON BALM

Step-by-Step Method

To install the hanging garden

1. Select a location to hang the shoe organizer. Hang it at a height where you are able to reach all the pockets. Here are some options for hanging:

    a. Hang the shoe organizer with the included hangers over a fence or wall. Just attach the hangers through the eyelets and place the brackets over the top of the fence or wall, the same way you would hang it from a door. The weight of all the soil and plants should keep it in place even when it's windy.

    b. Using the drill fitted with a screwdriver bit, attach the shoe organizer to a shed or house wall or a fence, with 3 screws through the eyelets. You may need to use appropriate drill bits and fasteners (not included in the materials and tools listed) if screwing into a stucco or cement wall. Use safety glasses when drilling.

    c. Hang the shoe organizer from an overhead beam of a porch or deck, either with the hangers or using the eyelets. Keep in mind that the shoe organizer is heavy, so make sure the beam can support the weight. You may also need to attach some string or chain at the bottom corners and tie them to a deck railing or other attachment point so the hanging garden won't become a swinging pendulum during heavy wind.

2. If you're hanging the shoe organizer against a vertical surface, attach the strip of wood with 2 deck screws close to where the bottom of the shoe organizer will be so it prevents excess water from dripping onto the surface and staining it.

3. Place the trough underneath the shoe organizer to catch water. Put it on the ground or mount it on the wall directly underneath the organizer.

To plant the garden

1. Fill each pocket with soil, leaving room at the top of each pocket so the soil doesn't spill out when adding plants.

2. Plant the strawberry, mint, and lemon balm plants in the pattern shown in the illustration (see page 119). Keep the crown (the part of the plant where the leaves come out) of the strawberry plants above the surface of the soil.

3. Water deeply. Top off any pockets with a bit of soil if the soil sinks after watering.

Care

Water the garden daily, adding water to each pocket with a watering can. Check for moisture levels by sticking your finger in the dirt or feeling the outside of the mesh. The soil should be damp. Every two weeks, water with a diluted liquid fertilizer, such as fish or seaweed or a mix.

Remove any dead leaves from the strawberry plants to keep them clean and tidy.

Once the strawberries are done, give them a haircut by cutting away excess growth. If any runners grow from the main plant, keep them to plant elsewhere or start another hanging garden.

Harvest

As the strawberries ripen, pick them. Pick the mint and lemon balm anytime. Cut whole stems with leaves. Cutting encourages bushier plants.

Substitution Tip: *Grow lettuce and greens instead of the strawberries and herbs in the hanging planter. Or grow only herbs to make it a hanging herb garden.*

CHAPTER 5

Indoor Gardening Projects

PROJECT 6
Windowsill Salad Garden

This super-simple project is the indoor equivalent of the Salad in a Container (see page 99), but without the tomato plants. This project takes up very little space because it sits on your windowsill, it doesn't require any artificial lighting, and if you place it in the kitchen, it's within easy reach while you're making a fresh salad. If your existing windowsill isn't at least 10 to 12 inches deep (most aren't), you'll need to make an easy modification with a pine board. You can have the lumberyard or home center cut the board to length for you. (It doesn't have to span the entire length of the sill.) Grow in recycled containers so you don't have to buy any planters, making this project even more cost-effective! Make sure you wear safety glasses when sawing and drilling.

Materials

1 (1-×-12-inch) pine board, cut to fit length of windowsill

#8 × 1¼-inch wood screws (number depends on length of board)

Sandpaper

Plastic, ceramic, or galvanized metal shallow drip tray(s) (12 inches wide max)

2 plastic, ceramic, terra-cotta, metal, or wood containers with drainage holes (at least 6 inches tall)

1 small bag sterilized potting soil

Organic liquid seaweed fertilizer

Tools

Measuring tape

Miter saw, circular saw, or handsaw (optional)

Safety glasses (optional)

Electric drill and ¹¹⁄₆₄-inch drill bit

Screwdriver bit to fit the wood screws

Spray bottle filled with water

Plants

1 package lettuce seeds, such as Grand Rapids or Salad Bowl

1 package basil seeds, such as sweet or Genovese

Step-by-Step Method

To install the windowsill garden

1. Carefully measure the windowsill to determine the length of the board.

2. If cutting lumber yourself, cut the boards to length with a saw. Wear safety glasses when sawing.

3. Using the drill and bit, drill a few holes in the face of the board, 2 inches in from each end and leaving about 6 inches between each hole. Place the board on the windowsill with the back of the board against the window trim.

4. Using the screws and drill fitted with the screwdriver bit, attach the board to the top of the windowsill.

5. Using sandpaper, sand the sharp edges from the front corners of the board to avoid injuries.

6. Place the drip tray(s) on the shelf.

To plant the garden

1. Fill each container with soil to about ½ inch from the rim.

2. In one container, sprinkle the lettuce seeds on top of the soil, following the package directions for spacing. You'll have leftovers to use later to replant.

3. In the other container, sprinkle the basil seeds on top of the soil, following the package directions for spacing. You'll have leftovers to use later to replant.

4. Cover the seeds with a thin layer (about ¼ inch) of soil.

5. Water well with the spray bottle.

Care

Keep your plants well-watered. If excess water drips out, empty the drip tray to reduce the humidity in your home. Every month, water the plants with a diluted fertilizer-water mix.

If you can, transfer the plants at night to a counter or table. If you leave them on the windowsill during very cold weather, they may get too cold—especially the basil. You also need to move them to fully close the blinds or other window coverings. Replace the plants if they stop producing well or seem sickly.

Harvest

To harvest the lettuce, pick the outer leaves first once the lettuce has a full set of leaves.

Basil thrives if you pick it regularly. Don't let the basil flower. If it does, pinch off the flowers to keep the leaves developing. Pick individual leaves or entire sprigs, which helps the basil become bushier.

Substitution Tip: *You can also grow other herbs and greens this way. Pick ones that won't grow too big for the windowsill's depth.*

PROJECT 7
Herb and Scallion Centerpiece

This easy-to-make centerpiece of herbs and scallions is a beautiful—and delicious!—showstopper for your dining table. Set out a few pairs of small scissors for your guests and have them snip a few fresh herbs to garnish their meals. You can get creative with the container you use and match it to your décor or the season. I don't recommend going larger than 6 × 12 inches; if your table is bigger, make two centerpieces. Unless your dining room gets lots of natural sunlight, store this centerpiece on a sunny windowsill, preferably in the kitchen, and move it to the dining room at mealtime.

Materials

1 (6-x-12-inch max) creative container, such as a galvanized trough, terra-cotta pot, miniature wooden crate, ceramic pot, or wicker basket with liner

1 saucer or drip tray to match container (see DIY Tip)

1 small bag sterilized potting soil

Organic liquid seaweed fertilizer

Tools

2 or 3 pairs of small scissors

Electric drill and 11/32-inch drill bit (optional)

Safety glasses (optional)

Spray bottle filled with water

Plants

1 package English thyme seeds

1 package oregano seeds, such as Greek or Italian

1 package basil seeds, such as sweet or Genovese

1 package Parade scallion seeds, or scallion roots for replanting

Step-by-Step Method

1. If your container doesn't have drainage holes, use the drill and bit to drill a few holes every 1 to 2 inches in the bottom. Use safety glasses while drilling.

2. Place the container on the drip tray.

3. Fill the container with soil to about ½ inch from the rim.

4. Sprinkle some thyme seeds along the edges of the pot. Sprinkle some oregano and basil seeds in a circle around the middle. Sprinkle a few scallion seeds in the middle or plant a scallion root in the middle, just covering the root but not the stalk.

5. Cover the seeds with a thin layer (about ¼ inch) of soil.

6. Water well with a spray bottle and keep the seeds damp until they sprout. Put some plastic wrap loosely on top of the container to help keep the seeds damp, especially if the air is very dry.

7. Once the seeds and scallion sprout, keep the centerpiece on a well-lit windowsill or in a bright location. If you don't have a sunny spot, place it under a grow light.

8. When you move the centerpiece to your dining room table for your guests, include scissors. Invite your guests to help themselves to the herbs and scallions, and give them the harvest instructions.

Care

Water weekly, keeping the soil damp. Make sure there is no standing water in the drip tray. Remove any dead branches from the herbs and fallen leaves from the container. Every month, replace one of the weekly waterings with an application of diluted fertilizer-water mix. Replace the scallion and basil plants if they stop producing well or seem sickly.

Harvest

As the herbs develop, snip off sprigs as needed or use individual leaves in your cooking. If you have the garden on your dining room table, your guests can do the same with the scissors.

Once the scallions are at least pencil thickness, snip off individual green leaves, leaving the smaller leaves at the base to grow.

DIY Tip: This project also works using the container-in-a-container method so you don't need any drip trays. Plant your herbs and scallion in small plastic pots (recycled yogurt or sour cream containers work well) that have drainage holes. Place the pots inside decorative containers and, if you wish, stuff some dried sphagnum moss (which you can buy in a craft shop) into the empty spots around the pots to hide the sides and top rim. Check the decorative containers for standing water and empty once in a while.

PROJECT 8
Microgreens for the Whole Family

This compact shelving unit provides 13½ square feet of microgreens in only 4½ square feet of floor space, tripling the amount of microgreens you can grow for your family! By using off-the-shelf LED lighting fixtures, you can put this project together in a weekend. You can add extra shelving units later if you need more greens or want to grow other vegetables or fruit, such as strawberries. Save money on this project by using recycled plastic deli containers. You'll need enough to fill all the shelves except the top one. Double up the containers so you don't need additional drip trays. If you don't have enough deli containers, use well-washed Styrofoam meat trays, lids from plastic containers, or shallow (10-x-20-inch) trays from a nursery or garden center.

Materials

1 (36-x-18-x-56-inch) metal or resin utility shelving unit with 4 ventilated or wire shelves

6 (2-foot) connectable LED grow lights

Several shallow deli containers with clear lids

Several shallow drip trays (optional)

2 to 3 cubic feet sterilized soil-less mix (see DIY Tip)

Plastic wrap (optional)

Tools

Sharp pencil or knife

Spray bottle filled with water

Plants

Several packages assorted seeds, such as arugula, amaranth, basil, beets, broccoli, kale, lettuce, purslane, spinach, Swiss chard, and wheat grass

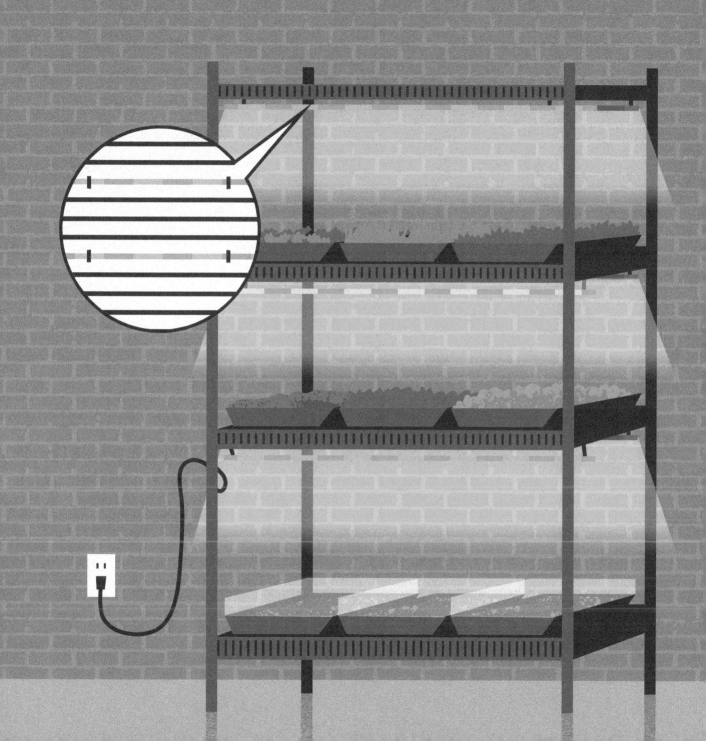

Step-by-Step Method

To set up the shelving unit

1. Assemble the shelving unit according to package directions.

2. Put the unit in its final location. Make sure this is near an electrical outlet.

3. Assemble the LED lighting fixtures and temporarily daisy-chain them together, plugging them in to make sure they all work.

4. Disconnect the lights and attach them (using the zip ties or clips that came with the lights) to the bottom of all the shelves except the bottom one. Position two lights parallel to each other on each shelf. Each pair of lights should be centered on the shelf from front to back and side to side. The light strips should be parallel to the long edges of the shelf with about 6 inches between them.

5. Reconnect the strips, then plug them in.

To prep the microgreens trays

1. Pair up each container with a second one, unless you are using drip trays. One container should nest into the other.

2. Prepare the interior container by poking some drainage holes in the bottom with the sharp pencil. Put the container with holes into the container without holes or on the drip trays (if using).

3. Fill the inner containers with the soil-less mix to about ½ inch from the rim.

4. Moisten the mix with the spray bottle, taking care not to overwater. If too much water ends up in the bottom container (or drip tray), empty the container.

To plant the microgreens

1. Sprinkle the assorted seeds onto the soil-less mix, following the package instructions for seed coverage. Spread them out with your hands if needed.

2. Sprinkle a fine layer of mix on top to just cover the seeds.

3. Water again with a fine spray to just dampen the seeds and added mix.

4. Cover the containers with their lid, or use plastic wrap if you don't have enough lids.

5. Place the containers on all the shelves except for the top one (you can use it to store light items, such as extra containers, tools, spray bottles, extra seeds, etc.).

6. Keep an eye on the containers, and when you see sprouts emerge, remove the lids or plastic wrap.

Care

Give the greens a light spray of water every day. If the bottom containers/drip trays fill with water, empty them.

Leave the lights on all day and night. If the lights disturb you at night, turn them off, but remember to turn them back on again when you wake up.

There is no need to fertilize the microgreens, as you'll eat them before they run out of nutrients from the seed.

Harvest

Once the microgreens are a couple of inches tall and before they start growing their larger leaves, harvest the leaves with a pair of sharp, clean kitchen scissors. Give them a quick rinse under running water and drain them.

Sometimes you can get a second crop, but usually you need to dispose of the roots and mix them into your compost or green recycling and start over again.

Alternatively, harvest the whole seedling with roots attached. Pull out a bunch of the seedlings, knocking off most of the mix. Give them a good rinse under running water to remove all mix and trim the roots before serving.

DIY Tip: *Although you can buy a sterilized soil-less mix, you can also mix your own fluffy mix, which may be less expensive. Use equal parts of vermiculite and either peat moss or coconut coir. Dampen all the ingredients well (you'll have to soak the coconut coir, as it usually comes in a compressed block) and mix them together.*

PROJECT 9
Tiered Veggie and Herbs Hanging Garden

This compact hanging garden makes use of an inexpensive set of wire hanging fruit baskets, easily purchased online or at home goods stores, to provide a space to grow some greens and herbs. It's an easy-to-construct project for a beginner. You can change up what you plant in each basket to suit your tastes. If you hang it in the kitchen, you'll have ready access to it as you cook and prepare food! This tiered hanger would also be great for strawberries, but they will likely need more light. Hang this in a room with a big window or a sunroom—or, better yet, in an outdoor space.

Materials
1 jumbo swag hook with hardware

1 drywall fastener (optional)

36 inches sturdy metal chain

1 (2- or 4-tiered) wire hanging fruit basket

3 (2-gallon) freezer bags

1 toothpick

1 small bag sterilized potting soil

1 plastic saucer slightly larger than the lowest basket

1 spool galvanized wire

Organic liquid seaweed fertilizer

Tools
Stud finder

Electric drill and ⅛-inch drill bit

Wire cutters and pliers

Scissors

Plants
3 lettuce seedlings, such as Little Gem and Red Salad Bowl

3 Bright Lights Swiss chard seedlings

1 creeping thyme seedling

1 holy basil seedling

1 cilantro seedling, such as Vietnamese or Santo (for seeds)

1 oregano seedling, such as Greek or Italian

Step-by-Step Method

To hang the baskets

1. Locate the hanging garden where it will get sunlight from a window or a skylight. Your kitchen would be the handiest location. Make sure it's not in a high-traffic area. Placing it in a corner of a room is best, as long it gets enough sunlight.

2. Ideally locate a ceiling structural support (called a joist) using the stud finder.

3. Using the drill and bit, drill a hole for the swag hook in the ceiling and screw it in. Ensure it is firmly mounted, as the hanger will be heavy. If you can't find a suitable structural support, use the drywall fastener (good swag hook kits provide a toggle bolt that works).

4. Hook the chain to the swag hook and hook the tiered baskets to the chain. Adjust the height of the chain at either the basket or the swag hook (by using different links) so you can easily reach each basket and still have room below on the floor.

To prepare the baskets and drip tray

1. Cut the freezer bags along the sides to create a flat plastic sheet. Cut the bags into a circle, cutting off the zip-top.

2. Fit the bags into the bottom of each basket. Don't worry about the excess.

3. Poke 3 or 4 holes in each bag liner at the bottom of the basket with the toothpick.

4. Fill each basket with soil to about ½ inch below the rim.

5. Drill 4 evenly spaced holes in the top edge of the plastic saucer.

6. Use lengths of wire to attach the saucer to the bottom basket to act as a drip tray. Make sure it is securely tied and that there are no stray wire ends that could poke someone. Make sure the tray is level so water doesn't spill out.

7. Water each basket until some water drips out the bottom. Make sure the drip tray can hold the excess water.

8. Trim the extra plastic around the tops of each basket.

To plant the garden

Plant the lettuce, herbs, and greens seedlings in each basket, keeping in mind that sometimes the lowest basket is deepest. Plant the seedlings that will have the most roots (the lettuce and chard) in the lowest basket. The thyme will hang down, so you can also plant that in the lowest basket so it doesn't shade the other plants.

Care

Water the soil in each basket until you see a few drops of water coming from the holes in the plastic bags. If the drip saucer gets full, carefully tip the water into a bucket or bowl to dispose of it. Every month, water with a diluted water-fertilizer mix. Remove any dead or rotting foliage as soon as you can.

Harvest

As leaves of the lettuce and greens get bigger, harvest individual leaves from the outside. Snip off herb sprigs or pluck off leaves as needed while cooking.

DIY Tip: *You could also hang the baskets on one of your walls, using a metal bracket like those used for hanging baskets outside. Make sure the hanger is firmly screwed into a wall stud or use the appropriate fasteners to carry the weight of the baskets.*

PROJECT 10
DIY Hydroponic Garden

Just think: You can have fresh tomatoes and cucumbers for salads in the comfort of your home without the mess of soil! This DIY hydroponic garden uses the Kratky method, which does not use any mechanical equipment to circulate water, making it the easiest method for a beginner. To make adding solution easier as your plants grow bigger, drill an extra hole in the lid. The hole should be large enough to fit a plastic funnel that you can use to top off the solution. When not in use, keep the hole covered with duct tape to avoid algae growth in the solution. It's important that your container keeps the light out, so make sure to choose one that is black or another dark color (or cover the container in black paint, plastic, or cloth).

Materials

4 (3-inch) net pots or plastic containers with holes poked into the bottoms and sides

1 (30-gallon) lidded black or dark-colored plastic storage tote

Complete liquid or granular hydroponic fertilizer

4 (2-inch) square rockwool cubes

1 small bag clay pebbles for hydroponic growing

1 jumbo swag hook with hardware

Duct tape

4 lengths strong string (long enough to span from the lid of the tote to the ceiling)

Tools

Permanent marker (such as a Sharpie)

Electric drill and ¹¹⁄₆₄-inch drill bit

Safety glasses

Thin handsaw (such as used for drywall) or electric saber saw

Coarse sandpaper or wood rasp/file

Measuring cup

Kitchen funnel

Plants

1 pack tomato seeds, such as Roma or Sweet Million

1 pack cucumber seeds, such as Patio Snacker

Step-by-Step Method

To prepare the storage tote

1. Set the bottom of the net pots on top of the storage tote's lid. Arrange them in a rectangle pattern, allowing enough space between the plants that will be growing.

2. Use the permanent marker to trace the bottom of the net pots onto the lid.

3. Using the drill and bit, drill a hole on the inside of each of the circles you drew. You may have to drill more than one hole side by side for the width of the saw you are using. Drill an additional hole in a corner of the lid. It should be wide enough to fit the bottom of a funnel, for adding solution later as the plants grow. Wear safety glasses when drilling.

4. Using the saw, carefully saw holes within the circles to create holes that are slightly smaller than the circles. These hold the net pots. You may need to use the sandpaper to enlarge the hole to fit the net pot.

5. Place the net pots in each hole so the lip of the pot keeps it from falling through the hole.

6. Rinse out the storage tote to get rid of the plastic chips from drilling and sawing.

7. Fill the tote with water, keeping track of how much water you're adding, until it covers the bottom of the net pots by 1 inch.

8. Make a mark with the permanent marker on the inside of the tote just above the level of the water.

9. Mix the appropriate amount of fertilizer into the water, following the instructions on the package. Granular fertilizer usually needs to be dissolved in a little bit of water before use. Once you have done this, pour the solution into the tote.

10. Snap the lid onto the tote.

To prepare the rockwool and plant seeds

1. Soak the rockwool cubes in water until well saturated.

2. Put 2 or 3 tomato or cucumber seeds in each cube. Two of the cubes are for tomatoes and two for cucumbers.

3. Place each cube into a net pot. Use the clay pebbles to keep the wool centered and stable in the pot, but also use them to cover the top to keep algae from growing, leaving enough space for the seedlings to emerge from the hole.

4. Place the net pots in the lid of the tote.

5. Once the seeds have germinated and the first sets of leaves are visible, gently pull out the weakest seedlings and keep the best one in each cube.

To add the support strings

1. Mount the swag hook on the ceiling above the middle of the tote according to package instructions.

2. Duct tape the strings to the lid of the tote, right beside each net pot.

3. Attach the other end of the strings to the swag hook and make sure they are taut. These provide support for the tomatoes and cucumbers as they grow.

Care

The Kratky method is, for the most part, a set-it-and-forget-it method. Usually, with greens like lettuce, you don't need to add more solution until it is used up. However, fruiting plants, such as tomatoes and cucumbers, need more time to grow and develop fruit. In this case, it's necessary to top off the solution occasionally. Check the tote every few weeks by lifting the lid carefully to see where the nutrient solution is. Check the permanent marker line you made on the inside of the tote when you first set it up. Once you see about 2 inches of free space between the mark and the water level, make another line with the marker. When the nutrient solution falls below that second mark, add more premixed solution up to that mark. Make sure the main plant roots are growing into the solution.

But make sure not to overfill! The plants produce regular roots that hang in the solution, but they also produce air roots that must remain outside of the solution, otherwise the plants literally drown. Soil has air pockets, but your solution doesn't.

You may have to add a grow light, depending on where you have placed your tote. Make sure the grow light is wide enough and tall enough to reach all of your plants, at least while they are still young. An adjustable height floor lamp works well. If there is a lot of natural light, you may not need additional light.

You may need to hand-pollinate your plants as mentioned in chapter 3 (see page 92). You can usually just lightly shake tomatoes and cucumbers by their branches each day to pollinate the flowers.

As the plants grow, simply guide the tendrils around the string. Be careful not to strangle the main stem of the plants by wrapping them too tightly around the string.

Harvest

Once the tomatoes and cucumbers are ripe, pick them. Wait for tomatoes to be the right color and slightly soft to the touch. You can usually pluck them off with a slight twist; make sure not to damage the branch. Pick cucumbers when they reach the size indicated on the package or seed catalog description. Pick frequently to promote more flowering and more cucumbers.

DIY Tip: *To make it easier to know when to add solution, take a thin, unfinished wood dowel that fits in the fill hole. When the nutrient solution is at the ideal level (see Care), put the dowel into the hole until it hits the bottom of the tote. Pull it out and make a mark with the permanent marker where the water level is (the damp part of the dowel). Next time you need to check the solution level, put the dowel into the hole until it hits the bottom and pull it out. If the damp part of the dowel has fallen below the mark you made, add solution.*

USDA GROWING ZONE MAP

This is the USDA map that shows the different grow zones in the United States. For information on grow zones outside of the United States, you can search online.

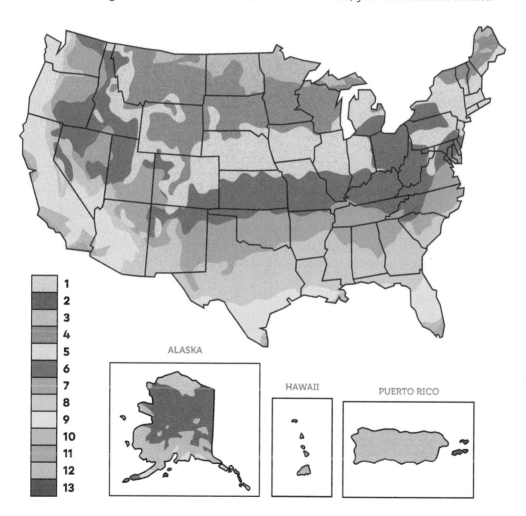

RESOURCES

Informational YouTube Channels

CaliKim Garden & Home DIY

https://www.youtube.com/channel/UCARXOI1UlItgIevoI5jZViQ

Information on both backyard and indoor growing.

Charles Dowding

https://www.youtube.com/channel/UCB1J6siDdmhwah7q0O2WJBg

A wealth of information on no-dig/no-till backyard growing.

David the Good

youtube.com/user/davidthegood

Videos and advice on natural growing.

Healthy Fresh Homegrown

https://www.youtube.com/channel/UCJhTZRtKq1l5rS5oaximHQA

Provides urban homestead tours and growing tips.

Khang Starr

youtube.com/user/KhangStarr010

Provides tutorials for many hydroponic projects.

Tikki O

https://www.youtube.com/channel/UCFxdiwy5rU7DBfQT6wnDm0A

Videos on Kratky method hydroponic as well as growing microgreens, sprouts, and more.

Books

Jamie at Home: Cook Your Way to the Good Life, *by Jamie Oliver*

One of my favorite cookbooks, with more than 100 tasty recipes for the produce you grow, plus some basic planting information and tips.

No Dig Organic Home & Garden: Grow, Cook, Use & Store Your Harvest

by Charles Dowding

An excellent book on no-dig organic gardening, which saves time and work. This type of garden requires an annual dressing of compost to help accelerate the improvement in soil structure and leads to higher fertility and fewer weeds.

A Year on the Garden Path: A 52-Week Organic Gardening Guide

by Carolyn Herriot

A weekly gardening guide with timely advice on how to create a beautiful, healthy, ornamental landscape and food garden. Full of helpful tips and recipes.

The Year-Round Vegetable Gardener: How to Grow Your Own Food 365 Days a Year, No Matter Where You Live, *by Niki Jabbour*

A great book on growing fresh, delicious produce, even in winter's coldest months.

The Zero-Mile Diet: A Year-Round Guide to Growing Organic Food

by Carolyn Herriot

This definitive month-by-month guide brings gardeners into the delicious world of edible landscaping and helps take a load off the planet as we work toward greater food security.

Informational Websites

Healthy Fresh Homegrown by Tranquil Urban Homestead

tranquilurbanhomestead.com

Dedicated to helping families with kids grow their own food at home. Information is structured as a three-year journey from a beginner garden to an urban homestead.

Garden Therapy

gardentherapy.ca

A website where you will find hundreds of garden-related projects, crafts, and recipes to help you live a better life through plants.

Old Farmer's Almanac

almanac.com

Since 1792, the Old Farmer's Almanac has spoken to all walks of life. And now it's online!

The Spruce

thespruce.com/world-hardiness-zones-3269822

This is a worldwide map of growing zones.

Seed Companies

Baker Creek Heirloom Seeds

rareseeds.com

Johnny's Selected Seeds

johnnyseeds.com

Renee's Garden

reneesgarden.com

Veseys

veseys.com

West Coast Seeds

westcoastseeds.com

Products/Suppliers

Lee Valley Tools

leevalley.com

A family-owned business that supplies gardening tools, woodworking tools, gifts, and household items through mail order or their stores in Canada.

Seeding Square

seedingsquare.com

An easy-to-use template that spaces seeds and seedlings correctly based on the type of plant.

Smart Pot

smartpots.com

The original award-winning fabric planter for faster-producing, healthier plants.

INDEX

S

Sage, 32–33
Salad in a Container, 99–101
Scale, 88
Scallions, 22–23, 83
Seedlings, 13, 16, 50–51
Seeds, 16
Seed starting, 52–54
Shovels, 36
Slugs, 60
Snails, 60
Soil amendments, 13, 14–15
Spider mites, 88
Spray bottles, 35
Strawberries, 26–27
Succession planting, 43, 85
Sun exposure, 13, 40, 61, 70

T

Terminology, 11–13
Thrips, 88
Thyme, 32–33
Tiered Veggie and Herbs
    Hanging Garden, 137–140
Tomatoes, 20–21
Tomato/tobacco hornworms, 60
Tools, 34–36
Transplants, 13
Triple mix soil, 14
Troubleshooting
  indoor gardens, 91–92
  outdoor gardens, 65–67
Trowels, 34
Turmeric, 84

U

Urban gardening. *See
    also* Indoor gardens;
    Outdoor gardens
benefits of, 4
fruits, 26–29
herbs, 30–33
locations, 9–10
organic, 4
steps, 5–6
tools, 34–36
types of, 8
vegetables, 20–25

V

Vegetables, 20–25
Ventilation, 71
Vertical and hanging gardens, 8
  Bin Bean Arbor, 114–117
  Hanging Drinks and Dessert
      Garden, 118–121
  indoor, 79
  maintenance, 47
  supports, 46–47
  Tiered Veggie and Herbs
      Hanging Garden, 137–140
  Wood Crate Tomato Planter
      with Support Cage, 109–113

W

Water, 15, 40, 55
Watering cans/hoses, 34
Watermelons, 28–29
Weather and elements, 61
Weeding, 56
White flies, 60

White mold (saprophytic
    fungus), 90
Wild animals, 64
Windowsill Salad Garden, 124–126
Wind protection, 40, 61
Wood Crate Tomato Planter with
    Support Cage, 109–113

Y

Yards, 10

Z

Zucchini, 20–21

ACKNOWLEDGMENTS

I would like to thank some key food growers, whom I consider my mentors and guides on my own homegrown good journey.

Charles Dowding from the United Kingdom has popularized the no-dig gardening method and his YouTube videos are delightful to watch and contain a wealth of information.

CaliKim from California is also a popular YouTuber who has brought homegrown food to beginners in a simple, easy-to-understand manner.

Local food grower Carolyn Herriot was my inspiration to garden organically, and I own two of her books. In addition to her valuable gardening advice, I love the tasty recipes she includes.

Showing that weather can't deter the most dedicated (some would say stubborn) food growers, Niki Jabbour from Halifax, Nova Scotia, Canada, is a fellow Canuck who has beaten the odds to grow vegetables year-round in some of the toughest conditions.

And, finally, thanks to my wife and daughter, who put up with my many hours at the computer writing this book!

ABOUT THE AUTHOR

 **MARC THOMA** is a father, husband, food grower, and woodworker who has more than 15 years of experience growing vegetables, fruit, herbs, and edible flowers at home. He lucked out when he was house-searching and found the perfect urban backyard with mature fruit trees, an established vegetable garden, and a lean-to greenhouse. He has worked hard to establish a thriving growing space that puts healthy, fresh food on his family's table and has developed his backyard into the Tranquil Urban Homestead, an escape from a busy 9-to-5 office job.

His passion for growing food and addressing the world's food and environmental problems culminated when he started the Tranquil Urban Homestead website and its Healthy Fresh Homegrown brand. On the website, he shares information on how to grow food at home. He's also active on various social media. For access to a free downloadable library of worksheets, cheat sheets, and checklists, sign up for his weekly email at tranquilurbanhomestead.com.